One Pan Perfect

fresh fast no-fuss deliciousness

Photography by Chris Court

ONE PAN PERFECT
Copyright © Donna Hay Pty Ltd 2021
Design copyright © Donna Hay Pty Ltd 2021
Photography copyright © Chris Court 2021
Recipes and styling: Donna Hay
Art direction and design: Chi Lam
Senior designer and Managing Editor : Hannah Schubert
Copy editor: Mariam Digges
Recipe testing: Jacinta Cannataci and Tina McLeish
dh Sponsorships and collaborations manager: Morgan Mathers
dh Digital strategist and producer: Lauren Gibb

Fourth Estate
An imprint of HarperCollins*Publishers*

HarperCollins*Publishers*
Australia • Brazil • Canada • France • Germany • Holland • Hungary
India • Italy • Japan • Mexico • New Zealand • Poland • Spain • Sweden
Switzerland • United Kingdom • United States of America

First published in Australia in 2021
by HarperCollins*Publishers* Australia Pty Limited
Level 13, 201 Elizabeth Street, Sydney NSW 2000
ABN 36 009 913 517
harpercollins.com.au

A catalogue record for this book is available from the National Library of Australia
ISBN 978 1 4607 6048 2

Reproduction by Hannah Schubert and Splitting Image
Printed and bound in Bosnia and Herzegovina by GPS Group on 140gsm Golden Sun Woodfree
6 5 4 3 2 1 21 22 23 24

donna hay

One Pan Perfect

fresh
fast
no-fuss
deliciousness

FOURTH ESTATE

Contents

After a **BIG YEAR OF COOKING**, we all want to find ways to *cook faster and smarter* than ever before. To sit back and let **BIG, PUNCHY FLAVOURS** do the heavy lifting with *just a single pan, pot, tray or dish.* **ONE PAN PERFECT** is the only book you need to help you prepare almost-instant, **ALL-IN-ONE MEALS** that are *super-delicious* and *better for you.* Think fast, **TASTY NEW TWISTS** on all your favourites, ready to *upflavour weeknight family dinners* and lazy weekend lunches. I've peppered this book with all the **TIPS AND TRICKS** to *boost your confidence* in the kitchen. Whenever you see this **QR CODE**  simply scan it with your phone and it will *bring my recipes to life* through a series of **INSTANT VIDEOS** that will lift your cooking game to new heights: *your own personal cooking coach!* This is fuss-free, all-in-one cooking at its absolute tastiest. **ENJOY!**

Kitchen Basics

Recipe Basics

Sometimes, it pays to go back to basics. From simple swaps to shopping tips, paying attention to the small things often equals cooking success.

LET'S START WITH THE BASICS

It might seem obvious, but so many people don't read the recipe before they start cooking. Before you pick up a chopping board or knife, it's always best to read the ingredients list and method, so you know what you'll need and what to expect. Whether you're a novice or an experienced cook, it always pays to get acquainted with a recipe before diving in.

DO YOUR PREP

It's called *mise en place* in the restaurant world. Prepping and chopping your ingredients is one of the easiest ways to streamline the cooking process. Whether it's finely dicing an onion, measuring ingredient quantities or washing and trimming your vegetables, getting your prep done makes following a recipe more enjoyable and fuss-free.

ALL ABOUT THE HEAT

Regular ovens only take around 10–15 minutes to hit their highest temperatures. Placing your prepped pan or tray into a cold or not-quite-hot-enough oven can mean the difference between a kitchen success or disaster. All ovens are different, so getting to know your oven's heat distribution and its little quirks before launching into a baking recipes is advisable. If you find that your oven doesn't like to play by the rules, it might be as simple as slightly adjusting the temperature or rotating your food halfway through cooking, to achieve the best result. When pre-heating your frying pan, it's best to do so with a dry, empty pan. I prefer to add the oil once the pan is hot, so the high heat doesn't change the flavour or characteristics of the oil, or prevent it from reaching its smoking point too quickly.

SET A TIMER

Life gets busy and distractions are ever-present, so it helps if you set a timer on your phone or use a kitchen timer, to reduce the guesswork and keep you on track. This is especially important during baking, when even a minute can make a world of difference.

SWITCH IT UP

Be confident with substituting ingredients if you don't have the right ones on hand. Quite often, something you already have in the pantry will do the job, like using dried chilli flakes in place of fresh chilli, or white wine vinegar instead of apple cider vinegar. You can also add 2 teaspoons baking powder to 1 cup plain flour to make self-raising (self-rising) flour, or substitute coconut sugar for brown sugar. There are so many swaps that won't drastically change a recipe, so trust your instincts, and make your pantry work harder for you.

MAKE A SHOPPING LIST

Now this isn't groundbreaking, but making a shopping list (and sticking to it!) can save time, money and the planet, all at once. By knowing what you need to buy in advance, you'll be better at keeping yourself on track while at the supermarket. Food wastage is a significant problem, so plan ahead and only buy ingredients that you know you will use. The planet will thank you for it!

GET MEASURING

I always recommend checking the size of your baking tins and pans when a recipe calls for specific dimensions. Using a dish or tin in the wrong size can often mean that a recipe won't turn out as expected. Getting your ruler out to measure the diameter of your tin will help prevent any unwelcome surprises when your creations emerge from the oven. We measure all of our tins and pans by the base, not the top.

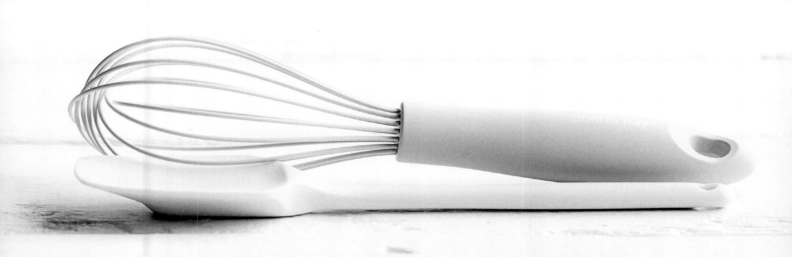

Tools and Prep

Starting with the right equipment makes all the difference. Sharp knives and a few clever tools ensure your prep is simpler, speedier and more enjoyable.

KNIVES

A good knife is your best friend in the kitchen. When buying a knife for yourself, look for one that fits your hand and grip. The weight of the knife should feel comfortable in your palm – it shouldn't feel too long. The best way to buy a knife is in person, so you can compare a few different brands and styles. If you're just starting out on your knife journey, a small starter set that includes a paring knife, serrated knife, and a utility or chef's knife, is a great place to begin.

PEELERS AND PREPPERS

Investing in good quality tools can make your life so much easier, and cut your kitchen prep time in half. Start with a sharp vegetable peeler, a mandoline, and a julienne peeler. These will help make light work of all your veggie prep in next to no time.

CHOPPING BOARDS

When it comes to choosing chopping boards, I like to have a variety of sizes on hand. Large chopping boards are perfect for prepping large quantities of vegetables, while small boards are great for a quick chop through some fresh herbs. To prevent your board from slipping around while you chop, place a small damp cloth or paper towel between the board and your benchtop. Wooden boards can quickly be refreshed by rubbing the surface with half a lemon and a generous sprinkle of salt.

MEASURE FOR SUCCESS

Before you get measuring, stock up on some cups for solid ingredients, jugs for liquid ingredients, and a set of kitchen scales for precision. Tablespoons vary from country to country, so check the guide on page 20 for the most accurate measurements.

SPEED IT UP

Food processors, blenders and stand mixers are my go-tos for chopping, whipping and mixing with speed. These appliances make prep time a breeze, and can do things in seconds that would take us mere mortals much longer. Gone are the days of slaving over a meringue with a whisk and bowl!

QUALITY IS KING

Investing in good quality cookware is so important. Not only are you purchasing something that will hopefully last you a lifetime, but you're saving money (and the planet!) by avoiding the need to re-purchase pots and pans after a year or so. High quality cookware often results in a more even cook, is super easy to clean, and will often feature ovenproof handles, perfect for travelling from stovetop to oven with ease.

BAKING ESSENTIALS

Not all cookware is created equal, and I have definitely discovered a few favourites over the years. For baking, you can't go past a 20cm (8 inch) round cake tin, a 20cm x 30cm (8 inch x 10 inch) square tin, and a 21cm x 10cm (8¼ inch x 4 inch) loaf tin, which should cover you from classic cakes and loaves through to delicious slices.

A FEW POTS AND PANS

Versatility is key when looking for cookware. A cast-iron skillet is the perfect vessel for achieving an even cook, every time. Deep baking dishes and trays will cover you for everything from lasagnes to puddings, while a Dutch oven or stockpot is a must-have for cooking large quantities, or letting flavours deepen over a slow simmer. And we can't forget the humble non-stick frying pan – need I say more about this kitchen (and clean up) saviour!

Tips and Tricks

There are always faster, better, more efficient ways to get ahead in the kitchen. Here are a few tricks I've learned along the way.

PEEL GARLIC WITH EASE

Now, this is a tip that will save you some serious time. Place a small handful of garlic cloves into a heavy-based jar and screw the lid on tightly. Shake the jar as hard as you can for a minute or so, until the cloves separate from their skins. Remove the garlic cloves from the jar and discard the skins, and you have peeled garlic, ready in a flash!

FRESH HERBS FOR LONGER

To extend the life of your delicate herbs, snip off the base of their stems and place the herbs into a cup or container that has been partially filled with water. Store them in the fridge and change the water as needed.

WRAP YOUR GREENS

Depending on your fridge, you might find that greens like spinach, silverbeet and kale lose their freshness after a day or two. To extend their lifespan and crisp texture, wrap your greens in a clean wet tea towel and store them in the crisper drawer of your fridge.

ICED WATER REVIVAL

It's so easy for herbs and salad leaves to lose their lustre and become limp and soggy. For a quick refresh, pop herbs and salad leaves into a bowl of iced water for a few minutes and watch them return to their fresh former selves. This trick is especially great when making a salad on a hot summer's day, or when serving food outdoors. A classic styling tip that makes such a difference!

PRESERVE AT ITS PEAK

There's no better time to take advantage of the freshest fruit and veggies than when they are in season. Freezing, pickling or preserving berries, fruits and vegetables while they're at their best (and cheapest) is a great way to ensure you always have the best produce on hand.

A CLEAN SLICE

If you've ever tried to cut through a slice that has come straight out of the fridge, this tip is for you. For a clean slice when cutting through chilled tray cakes, semifreddo or slices, run the blade of a chef's knife under a hot tap until the surface is warm, but not hot, to the touch. Then, cut into your chilled treats with ease and carefully wipe the blade between cuts. You can warm your knife again as needed between each slice, to achieve a perfectly clean cut every time.

THE SHARP EDGE

It might sound obvious, but keeping your knives sharp will cut some serious time off your prep. And there's nothing quite like the sheer joy of chopping, slicing or dicing with a sharp knife. If you aren't feeling confident enough to sharpen your own knives, most kitchenware stores will provide the service.

PICTURE-PERFECT PASTA

This is my styling tip for serving the perfect plate of pasta. When your pasta is ready (this trick works for long varieties, like spaghetti or linguini), pick up a portion with a pair of tongs. Meanwhile, use your other hand to continuously spin your serving plate on a bench or tabletop while you carefully release the pasta onto the plate in a perfectly coiled nest. This clever trick will help your pasta sit up with more altitude and attitude!

Shortcuts and Time-savers

I'm always looking for ways to make my freezer, pantry and everyday kitchen tools work harder for me, especially during those busy midweek nights.

DEEP FREEZE

You should think of your freezer as a second pantry. I try to keep mine full of useful ingredients, ready to create something magical at the drop of a hat. Ready-rolled pastry or cookie dough, plain sponge cake, wonton wrappers, and breadcrumbs are the perfect base for a delicious creation, while edamame beans, chopped kale, spinach and stock are ready and waiting to give your next meal a nourishing twist.

Freezing cooked rice, quinoa or pasta for a rapid-fire meal or side is a clever way to plan ahead for busy weeknights. Flavour saviours like kaffir lime leaves or curry leaves are also great to freeze and upflavour a dish at a moment's notice. Leftover stock or citrus juices can be frozen in small quantities in ice-cube trays or small containers. And there's always room on a freezer shelf for some ice-cream and frozen yoghurt to team with something freshly baked!

EASY CLEAN

Baking paper is a kitchen lifesaver. It's perfect for lining trays and baking dishes, and it's also my number one tool for reducing time spent on washing up. Plus, it does wonders for locking in all of those delicious flavours in the pan. Pick up the edges of the paper and bring them together to capture delicious pan juices and sauces, or crimp the paper around your ingredients to seal in steam. As a plus, you can also buy bleach-free, home compostable brown baking paper that is a win for the planet, too.

TAKE THE SNIP

If chopping with a knife just isn't your thing, a pair of heavy-duty kitchen scissors works a treat chopping fresh herbs, chilli and green onions in a flash.

SHORTCUTS TO FLAVOUR

Having your favourite condiments and pastes on hand can often be the difference between a meal that falls flat or sings with flavour. The addition of mustard in a dressing or miso stirred through mayonnaise can really lift your final dish. Don't be afraid to put your condiments into hyper-drive by experimenting with different flavours.

FLAVOUR BASES

If you're looking to build some big flavour starters to keep on standby, look no further than Chapter 5, where you'll discover a zingy *red chilli coconut paste*, a rich, silky *confit garlic*, and more. It's just what you need in your fridge to add some big punchy flavours to your next meal – my super tasty 'just add fresh' meal solutions.

Cooking Seasonally and Pantry Staples

Starting with fresh, quality produce, adding a few simple ingredients and cooking them without fuss, has always been my mantra.

GET SEASONAL

In-season fruits and vegetables are at their absolute peak in terms of texture and flavour. They also cost less because of their abundant availability. By choosing recipes that feature seasonal produce, you are starting ahead of the game when it comes to taste. Visit your local farmer's markets to support local farmers and producers and help reduce the distance your food travels from farm to table, which is great for the farmer, for you (hello, fresher-than-fresh produce!), and for the planet. My recipes for *any fruit tart* on page 54 and *any fruit coconut crumble* on page 142 make the most of all the seasons. You can find some delicious flavour combinations at the bottom of each page, but don't be afraid to create your own, either. The possibilities are endless! Just look to the season for inspiration.

BETTER-FOR-YOU PANTRY STAPLES

FLOURS - Ingredients that lift the nutritional content of your baked goods are becoming more readily available in supermarkets. Flours such as wholemeal (whole-wheat), spelt, buckwheat and coconut can all be used in varying quantities, depending on their density. Swapping a cup for a cup with plain flour can be tricky, so start by swapping ½-cup ratios and see how you go.

SUGARS - Switch regular sugars for more naturally processed sugars, such as coconut, rapadura, raw, pure maple syrup, or agave syrup. These sweet alternatives contain more trace minerals than their more traditional counterparts. They can't always be swapped cup for cup, so start with a small portion from the recipe and experiment as you go.

SEEDS AND NUTS - These are the real powerhouses to add to your baked goods, pastas and salads. Not only do they offer crunch, but they are a super simple way to nutritionally uplift your favourite dishes. A few favourites you'll find in this book are omega 3-rich chia seeds, protein and vitamin-packed hemp seeds, plus almonds and cashews (as either whole nuts or butters). Some seeds you'll come across include pepitas (pumpkin seeds), sunflower seeds and sesame seeds (also featured in paste-form as tahini). These are all wonderful sources of vitamins and antioxidants. It's so simple to sprinkle a few chia seeds into your next crumble topping, or to use a nut butter to bind your next slice base or decadent cake frosting together.

BEANS AND LENTILS - Your pantry is not complete without a can or two of white (cannellini) beans, chickpeas, or lentils. Filled with essential vitamins, minerals and protein, these user-friendly options require no pre-soaking or cooking. They're not only the heroes in your pantry, but they'll also be the hero of many dishes.

RICE - Try switching regular rice for brown or black rice. These easy, nutritious swaps will up the protein and antioxidants in your food, not to mention add some textural fun to your regular rice bowl.

TOFU - This underrated ingredient is a great, protein-rich vegetarian stand-in for meat. Both silken and firm tofu can be used in savoury dishes such as stir-fries, soups, or my super-tasty *pumpkin tofu burgers with herb mayonnaise* (see page 92). Tofu can also be used to create a creamy mayonnaise or mousse-based dessert.

OILS - There is always much debate over which oil to use. The following is what I like to do. I much prefer the health benefits of a fresh extra virgin olive oil over other oils. When I need a neutral tasting oil for baking or when I'm cooking Asian dishes, I like to use a light-flavoured extra virgin olive oil. I swap between robust and deep-flavoured extra virgin olive oils, depending on what I'm cooking. On the occasion I need a very neutral oil, I prefer to use a cold-pressed vegetable or seed-based oil.

global measures

Measures vary from Europe to the US and even from Australia to New Zealand.

metric and imperial

Measuring cups and spoons may vary slightly from one country to another, but the difference is generally not sufficient to affect a recipe. The recipes in this book use Australian measures. All cup and spoon measures are level. An Australian measuring cup holds 250ml (8½ fl oz).

One Australian metric teaspoon holds 5ml (⅛ fl oz), one Australian tablespoon holds 20ml (¾ fl oz) (4 teaspoons). However, in the USA, New Zealand and the UK, 15ml (½ fl oz) (3-teaspoon) tablespoons are used.

When measuring dry ingredients, add the ingredient loosely to the cup and level with a knife. Don't tap or shake to compact the ingredient unless the recipe requests 'firmly packed'.

liquids and solids

Measuring cups, spoons and scales are great assets in the kitchen – these equivalents are a guide.

liquids

cup	metric	imperial
⅛ cup	30ml	1 fl oz
¼ cup	60ml	2 fl oz
⅓ cup	80ml	2¾ fl oz
½ cup	125ml	4¼ fl oz
⅔ cup	160ml	5½ fl oz
¾ cup	180ml	6 fl oz
1 cup	250ml	8½ fl oz
2 cups	500ml	17 fl oz
3 cups	750ml	25 fl oz
4 cups	1 litre	34 fl oz

solids

metric	imperial
20g	¾ oz
60g	2 oz
125g	4½ oz
180g	6¼ oz
250g	8¾ oz
450g	1 lb
750g	1 lb 10 oz
1kg	2 lb 3 oz

more equivalents

Here are a few more simplified equivalents for metric and imperial measures, plus ingredient names.

millimetres to inches

metric	imperial
3mm	⅛ inch
6mm	¼ inch
1cm	½ inch
2.5cm	1 inch
5cm	2 inches
18cm	7 inches
20cm	8 inches
23cm	9 inches
25cm	10 inches
30cm	12 inches

ingredient equivalents

almond meal	ground almonds
bicarbonate of soda	baking soda
caster sugar	superfine sugar
celeriac	celery root
chickpeas	garbanzo beans
coriander	cilantro
cornflour	cornstarch
cos lettuce	romaine lettuce
eggplant	aubergine
gai lan	chinese broccoli
green onion	scallion
icing sugar	confectioner's sugar
plain flour	all-purpose flour
rocket	arugula
self-raising flour	self-rising flour
silverbeet	swiss chard
snow pea	mange tout
white sugar	granulated sugar
zucchini	courgette

oven temperatures

Setting the oven to the correct temperature can be crucial when baking sweet things.

celsius to fahrenheit

celsius	fahrenheit
100°C	200°F
120°C	250°F
140°C	275°F
150°C	300°F
160°C	325°F
180°C	350°F
190°C	375°F
200°C	400°F
220°C	425°F

electric to gas

celsius	gas
110°C	¼
130°C	½
140°C	1
150°C	2
170°C	3
180°C	4
190°C	5
200°C	6
220°C	7
230°C	8
240°C	9
250°C	10

butter and eggs

Let 'fresh is best' be your mantra when it comes to selecting eggs and dairy goods.

butter

We generally use unsalted butter as it allows for a little more control over a recipe's flavour. Either way, the impact is minimal. Salted butter has a longer shelf life and is preferred by some people. One American stick of butter is 125g (4½ oz). One Australian block of butter is 250g (8¾ oz).

eggs

Unless otherwise indicated, we use large (60g/2 oz) chicken eggs. To preserve freshness, store eggs in the refrigerator in the carton they are sold in. Use only the freshest eggs in recipes such as mayonnaise or dressings that use raw or barely cooked eggs. Be extra cautious if there is a salmonella problem in your community, particularly in food that is to be served to children, pregnant women or the elderly.

useful weights

Here are a few simple weight conversions for cupfuls of commonly used ingredients.

common ingredients

almond meal (ground almonds)
1 cup | 120g | 4¼ oz
brown sugar
1 cup | 175g | 6 oz
raw caster (superfine) sugar
1 cup | 220g | 7¾ oz
coconut sugar
1 cup | 150g | 5¼ oz
desiccated coconut
1 cup | 80g | 2¾ oz
**plain (all-purpose)
or self-raising (self-rising) flour**
1 cup | 150g | 5¼ oz
raw or roasted cashews
1 cup | 150g | 5¼ oz
finely grated parmesan
1 cup | 80g | 2¾ oz
uncooked brown rice
1 cup | 200g | 7 oz
cooked brown rice
1 cup | 165g | 5¾ oz
cooked quinoa
1 cup | 140g | 5 oz
fresh or frozen berries
1 cup | 125g | 4½ oz
**finely shredded firmly packed
kale leaves**
1 cup | 35g | 1¼ oz

chapter one
One Tray

There's so MUCH TO LOVE about a *one-tray wonder*! These easy, breezy meals are *so simple* and SUPER TASTY thanks to all those *beautiful tray juices* doing the HEAVY LIFTING while you *sit back and relax*. All that's left to do is prep, SET AND FORGET – your oven takes *care of the rest*, letting all those FRESH INGREDIENTS cosy up to each other, *caramelise and concentrate* into a new LEVEL OF YUM. Less labour, *more flavour.*

This EXPRESS CHICKEN and haloumi bake leaves
you with a *gorgeous pool* of SWEET, CITRUSY, HERBY
tray juices to drag *each bite through*.

chicken with burnt lemons and haloumi

12 sprigs marjoram or oregano
2 lemons, cut into six wedges each
2 tablespoons extra virgin olive oil
4 x small 180g chicken breast fillets, trimmed
200g haloumi, sliced
2 tablespoons honey
sea salt and cracked black pepper
4 cups (100g) baby spinach leaves

Preheat oven to 220°C (425°F).

Place the marjoram and lemons on a large baking tray
lined with non-stick baking paper and drizzle with oil.

Bake for 20 minutes or until the lemons start to char
on the edges. Add the chicken to the tray and roll in
the tray juices to coat. Top with haloumi and drizzle
with honey. Sprinkle with salt and pepper and bake for
12–15 minutes or until the chicken is cooked through.

To serve, place spinach leaves onto serving plates and
top with the hot chicken, haloumi and lemons to slightly
wilt the spinach. Spoon the tray juices over the top and
serve. **SERVES 4**

*This chicken makes
a tasty baguette
filling the next day.*

SCAN THIS CODE FOR RECIPE VIDEO

Crunchy golden chicken is always a GOOD IDEA.
This *super-charged* version is loaded with
FLAVOUR-RICH miso and nutty toasted pepitas.

pepita-crusted chicken with avocado and edamame salad

3 egg whites
2 tablespoons white (shiro) miso paste
sea salt and cracked black pepper
1½ cups (240g) pepitas (pumpkin seeds),
   finely chopped
3 x 180g small chicken breast fillets,
   halved horizontally
extra virgin olive oil, for drizzling
avocado and edamame salad
¼ cup (60ml) extra virgin olive oil
2 tablespoons rice wine vinegar
1 tablespoon white (shiro) miso paste
1 tablespoon water
4 cups (60g) mizuna leaves (Japanese mustard greens)[+]
1 cup (16g) coriander (cilantro) leaves
1 large avocado, quartered
1 cup (140g) frozen shelled edamame beans, blanched
   and cooled

Preheat oven grill (broiler) to high.

Place the egg whites, miso, salt and pepper in a bowl and whisk to combine. Place the pepitas on a flat plate.

Dip the chicken into the egg mixture, then gently press both sides into the pepitas to coat. Place chicken on a large baking tray lined with non-stick baking paper and drizzle generously with oil.

Grill for 4–5 minutes each side, until the pepitas are crunchy and golden and the chicken is cooked through.

To make the avocado and edamame salad, combine the oil, rice wine vinegar, miso and water in a large bowl. Add the mizuna leaves, coriander, avocado and edamame beans and toss gently to coat in the dressing.

Serve the pepita-crusted chicken with the avocado and edamame salad. **SERVES 4**

+ *If you can't find mizuna, use any mustard greens or rocket (arugula) leaves.*

Salty–sweet miso takes this chicken to a new level of yum!

Who can turn down **IRRESISTIBLE BAKED CHEESE,**
with its golden top and *gooey centre?* It stars here in
a new riff on the **CLASSIC ITALIAN** panzanella salad.

baked tomato and eggplant salad

500g (about 4) Japanese finger eggplants
  (aubergines), quartered and sliced
700g cherry tomatoes
sea salt and cracked black pepper
2 x 200g pieces smooth feta
2 tablespoons extra virgin olive oil, plus extra
  for brushing
250g (about 3 thick slices) torn sourdough bread
8 sprigs oregano
½ cup (8g) mint leaves
½ cup (12g) flat-leaf (Italian) parsley leaves
½ cup (10g) basil leaves
dressing
¼ cup (60ml) extra virgin olive oil
¼ cup (60ml) red wine vinegar

Preheat oven to 200°C (400°F).

To make the dressing, combine the oil and vinegar.
Set aside.

Place the eggplant, cherry tomatoes, salt, pepper and
half the dressing into a large bowl and toss to coat.

Place the feta in the centre of a large baking tray lined
with non-stick baking paper and arrange the tomatoes
and eggplant around it.

Brush the feta with oil and bake for 20–22 minutes or
until the tomatoes start to blister.

In a separate bowl, combine the bread, oregano and
oil and toss to coat. Place the bread and oregano mix on
top of the tomatoes and bake for a further 8–10 minutes
or until golden. Serve with mint, parsley and basil, and
drizzle with the reserved dressing. **SERVES 4**

This is a great way to give old bread a new life.

I love this combination of CARAMELISED ROAST PUMPKIN, smoky chorizo and *earthy chickpeas*, refreshed with BRIGHT GREEN kale leaves.

roasted pumpkin and chorizo salad with crispy chickpeas and feta

1.2kg butternut pumpkin, seeds removed and
  cut into large chunks
1 x 400g can chickpeas (garbanzo beans),
  rinsed and drained
8 sprigs sage
420g (about 3) chorizo sausages, thickly sliced
¼ cup (60ml) sherry vinegar
5 cups (175g) firmly packed shredded kale leaves
200g feta, broken into large chunks
1 cup (24g) flat-leaf (Italian) parsley leaves
lemon wedges, to serve
marinade
⅓ cup (120g) honey
⅓ cup (80ml) extra virgin olive oil
1 tablespoon sweet smoked paprika
sea salt and cracked black pepper

Preheat oven to 220°C (425°F).

To make the marinade, combine the honey, oil, paprika, salt and pepper.

Place the pumpkin, chickpeas, and sage onto a large baking tray lined with non-stick baking paper. Pour half the marinade over the top and toss to coat.

Bake for 30 minutes, then add the chorizo and bake for a further 15 minutes, or until the pumpkin is cooked and caramelised.

To make the dressing, combine the sherry vinegar and reserved marinade.

In a large bowl, scrunch the kale and dressing together with your hands for 2 minutes.

Serve the pumpkin and chickpeas with the kale, feta, parsley and lemon wedges. **SERVES 4**

Feel free to use any in season pumpkin you can find.

Your favourite nutty, creamy Asian TAKE AWAY STAPLE is now a *speedy one-tray* wonder, with cashews and broccolini for a BETTER-FOR-YOU twist.

cashew satay chicken skewers with chilli ginger broccolini

700g (about 12) broccolini (sprouting broccoli), trimmed
¼ cup (60ml) extra virgin olive oil
3 teaspoons finely grated ginger
1 long red chilli, finely chopped
750g chicken breast fillets, trimmed and cut into 2cm (¾ inch) pieces
green onion (scallion), coriander leaves (cilantro) and kecap manis (sweet soy sauce), to serve
cashew satay
1 cup (150g) finely chopped roasted salted cashews
1 cup (250ml) coconut cream
2 tablespoons lime juice
1 tablespoon fish sauce
1 tablespoon finely grated ginger
1 teaspoon ground cumin

Preheat oven to 220°C (425°F).

Place the broccolini in 4 piles on a baking tray lined with non-stick baking paper. Combine the oil, ginger and chilli and spoon over the broccolini.

To make the cashew satay, combine the cashews, coconut cream, lime juice, fish sauce, ginger and cumin in a bowl. Add the chicken and toss to coat. Thread chicken onto metal skewers.

Place the chicken on top of the broccolini and pour any remaining cashew satay over the top.

Bake for 15–20 minutes or until the broccolini is tender and the chicken is cooked through.

Serve with green onions, coriander and a drizzle of kecap manis. SERVES 4

Use peanuts instead of cashews if you have them on hand.

HOMEMADE FALAFEL doesn't have to be an *all-day project!* This SPEEDY VERSION is loaded with shortcuts and nourishing, *spice-fuelled ingredients.*

turmeric carrot falafel with minted yoghurt

1 x 400g can white (cannellini) beans, rinsed and drained

1 onion, finely chopped

3 cups (360g) peeled and grated carrot

¼ cup (50g) white chia seeds

2 cups (70g) firmly packed finely shredded kale leaves

1 cup (16g) coriander (cilantro) leaves

½ cup (8g) mint leaves

2 teaspoons ground or fresh grated turmeric

½ teaspoon baking powder

sea salt and cracked black pepper

extra virgin olive oil, for brushing

cos (romaine) lettuce leaves, vine-ripened tomatoes, mint and sumac, to serve

minted yoghurt

1 cup (280g) plain thick yoghurt

2 tablespoons finely chopped mint leaves

1 tablespoon lemon juice

Preheat oven to 220°C (425°F).

Place the beans, onion, carrot, chia, kale, coriander, mint, turmeric, baking powder, salt and pepper into a food processor and process until finely chopped.

Shape ¼ cupfuls of the mixture into patties and place on a large baking tray lined with non-stick baking paper. Brush the patties generously with oil and bake for 25–30 minutes or until golden.

While the falafel are cooking, make the minted yoghurt by mixing the yoghurt, mint and lemon juice together.

Serve the falafel with lettuce, tomatoes, mint, sumac and minted yoghurt. MAKES 16

These falafel make the perfect portable picnic lunch!

I love the simplicity of this HEARTY TRAY BAKE, which capitalises on *a few star ingredients* that create LAYERS OF FLAVOUR in moments.

chicken, chorizo and potato tray bake

1kg roasting potatoes, peeled and sliced into
   thin wedges
2 red onions, peeled and sliced into wedges
¼ cup (60ml) extra virgin olive oil
sea salt and cracked black pepper
4 x 125g chicken thigh fillets, trimmed and halved
3 chorizo sausages, cut into thirds
1 tablespoon sweet smoked paprika
8 sprigs oregano
2 tablespoons pure maple syrup
4 stalks kale (110g), stems removed, leaves torn

Preheat oven to 220°C (425°F).

Place the potatoes, onion, 2 tablespoons oil, salt and pepper in a bowl and toss to coat. Place on a large baking tray lined with non-stick baking paper and bake for 20–25 minutes or until lightly golden.

While the potatoes are cooking, combine the chicken, chorizo, paprika, oregano, maple syrup and remaining oil and toss to coat.

Place the kale on top of the potatoes, top with the chicken and chorizo mixture and cook for a further 20–25 minutes or until the chicken is golden and cooked through. SERVES 4

Keep the chorizo pieces nice and big to stop them from burning.

SCAN THIS CODE FOR RECIPE VIDEO

This salad is loaded with FLAVOUR AND TEXTURE.
There's *tang from the capers*, heat from the chilli
and creaminess from the feta. SO GOOD!

charred broccoli studio salad

½ cup (125ml) extra virgin olive oil
3 long red chillies, deseeded and shredded
⅓ cup (60g) salted baby capers, rinsed
2 tablespoons finely grated lemon rind
4 cloves garlic, thinly sliced
4 heads broccoli, quartered
350g firm feta, cut into large chunks
120g wild rocket (arugula)
2 tablespoons extra virgin olive oil
2 tablespoons lemon juice
cracked black pepper
finely grated parmesan and lemon wedges, to serve

Preheat oven to 220°C (425°F).

Combine the oil, chillies, capers, lemon rind and garlic in a bowl. Place the broccoli onto a large baking tray lined with non-stick baking paper. Pour the chilli caper mixture over the broccoli to coat it.

Bake for 20 minutes, then add the feta to the tray and bake for a further 10 minutes or until the broccoli is charred on the edges.

Toss the rocket, oil, lemon juice and pepper together and scatter over the broccoli.

Top the broccoli, feta and rocket salad with the pan juices and serve with parmesan and lemon wedges.
SERVES 4

You can wrap this salad in warm flatbread with hummus.

A TASTY TRIO of panko, quinoa and chia seeds
gives these schnitzels a *shattering crunch,*
not to mention NUTRITIONALLY UPSCALES them.

crispy chia chicken schnitzels

4 x 180g small chicken breast fillets, trimmed
   and halved horizontally
2 teaspoons sweet smoked paprika
½ teaspoon chilli flakes
sea salt and cracked black pepper
2 tablespoons chia seeds
1 cup (100g) quinoa flakes
1 cup (60g) panko crumbs
2 egg whites, lightly whisked
light-flavoured extra virgin olive oil, for drizzling
baguettes and mayonnaise, to serve
pickled slaw
½ small wombok (Chinese cabbage), shredded
1 carrot, peeled and shredded
4 radishes, sliced into wedges
½ cup (8g) mint leaves
2 tablespoons apple cider vinegar
1 teaspoon honey
sea salt and cracked black pepper

Preheat oven grill (broiler) to high and place a baking tray
in the oven to heat up.

To make the schnitzels, sprinkle both sides of the
chicken with paprika, chilli, salt and pepper.

Place the chia, quinoa and panko crumbs in a bowl and
mix to combine.

Dip the chicken into the whisked egg whites, then press
firmly into the chia mixture to coat. Remove the hot tray
from the oven and place a sheet of non-stick paper onto
it. Top with the chicken and drizzle generously with oil.

Grill for 7–8 minutes or until the crust is golden and the
chicken is cooked through. Keep warm.

To make the pickled slaw, place the cabbage, carrot,
radish and mint in a bowl and toss to combine. Mix the
apple cider vinegar, honey, salt and pepper together.
Toss the slaw through the dressing to coat.

Serve the schnitzels with the pickled slaw, baguette
and mayonnaise. SERVES 4

You can leave out the chilli flakes if you prefer, and you can serve this without the baguette.

Haloumi and honey lend these fritters an ADDICTIVE SALTY-SWEETNESS. These golden *puffs of goodness* are JUST AS TASTY in a wrap as they are in a salad.

chickpea and cauliflower fritters

1 x 400g can chickpeas (garbanzo beans),
   rinsed and drained
3 cups (390g) firmly packed grated cauliflower
250g haloumi, grated
½ cup (28g) chopped mint leaves
½ cup (26g) chopped flat-leaf (Italian) parsley leaves
1 teaspoon ground turmeric
1 tablespoon finely grated lemon rind
2 tablespoons honey
3 eggs
2 tablespoons chia seeds
sea salt and cracked black pepper
extra virgin olive oil, for brushing
warm pita bread, salad and mint leaves,
   to serve
yoghurt dressing
1 cup (280g) plain thick yoghurt
½ teaspoon ground cumin
1 tablespoon lime juice

Preheat oven to 200°C (400°F).

To make the fritters, place the chickpeas into a large bowl and mash lightly. Add the cauliflower, haloumi, mint, parsley, turmeric, lemon rind, honey, eggs, chia seeds, salt and pepper and mix to combine.

Shape ¼ cupfuls into patties and place on a large baking tray lined with non-stick baking paper. Brush the patties with oil and bake for 25 minutes or until crisp and golden.

To make the yoghurt dressing, mix the yoghurt, cumin and lime juice together in a small bowl to combine.

Serve the fritters with the yoghurt dressing, pita bread, salad and mint leaves. **MAKES 16**

Use wet hands to help you shape these fritters.

You've never met MUSHROOMS LIKE THESE before! *They're so crisp* and pack a serious FLAVOUR PUNCH thanks to the *toasty blend* of spices.

crispy mushroom tacos with avocado and lime yoghurt

½ cup (125ml) extra virgin olive oil, plus extra
   for brushing
1 tablespoon sweet smoked paprika
1 teaspoon chilli flakes
sea salt and cracked black pepper
1kg portobello mushrooms, sliced into
   5mm (¼ inch) pieces
4 fresh jalapeño chillies, halved and seeds removed
2 cups (180g) finely shredded white cabbage
½ cup (8g) coriander (cilantro) leaves, torn
1 avocado, sliced
8 x 15cm (6 inch) flour tortillas, to serve
lime yoghurt
1 cup (280g) plain thick yoghurt
2 teaspoons finely grated lime rind
2 tablespoons lime juice
sea salt and cracked black pepper

Preheat oven to 240°C (475°F).

Place the oil, smoked paprika, chilli, salt and pepper in a large bowl and mix to combine. Add the mushrooms and gently mix to coat. Place on a large baking tray lined with non-stick baking paper. Brush the jalapeño chillies with a little oil and add to the tray. Bake for 45 minutes, stirring occasionally, until the mushrooms are crispy.

To make the lime yoghurt, place the yoghurt, lime rind, lime juice, salt and pepper in a bowl and mix to combine.

Divide the cabbage, coriander, avocado and lime yoghurt between the tortillas. Top with the mushrooms and jalapeño chillies and serve. **SERVES 4**

These mushrooms make a delicious 'meaty' taco filling!

This is a light, bright way to FEED A HOUSE, fast.
The combo of *crisp cauliflower,* JAMMY LEEKS
and feta blanketed in *herby dressing* is perfection.

crispy cauliflower salad with green tahini dressing

900g cauliflower florets
1 leek, cut into thick strips
¼ cup (60ml) extra virgin olive oil
¼ cup (4g) oregano leaves
sea salt and cracked black pepper
200g feta, cut into large chunks
2 Lebanese cucumbers, sliced
300g green beans, blanched and sliced
1 cup (24g) flat-leaf (Italian) parsley leaves
1 cup (16g) mint leaves
warm flatbread, to serve
green tahini
¾ cup (210g) hulled tahini
½ cup (125ml) lemon juice
½ cup (125ml) water, plus extra if needed
1 cup (16g) mint leaves
1 cup (24g) flat-leaf (Italian) parsley leaves
sea salt and cracked black pepper

Preheat oven to 220°C (425°F).

Place the cauliflower and leek on a large baking tray lined with non-stick baking paper. Add the oil, oregano, salt and pepper and toss to combine.

Bake for 30 minutes, then add the feta and toss to combine. Bake for a further 10 minutes or until golden and crisp. Set aside to cool slightly.

To make the green tahini, place the tahini, lemon juice, water, mint, parsley, salt and pepper in a small food processor or blender and blend until smooth.

Toss the cauliflower, cucumbers, beans, parsley and mint together. Top with the green tahini and serve with warm flatbread. **SERVES 4**

Swap the beans for any crunchy greens you have on hand.

chapter one

One Tray

sweet

Presenting EVERYTHING YOU LOVE about carrot cake in a big, *crisp-on-the-outside*, SOFT-ON-THE-INSIDE, lemon cream cheese-frosted cookie! *You're welcome.*

carrot cake cookies with cream cheese frosting

1 cup (90g) rolled oats

1 cup (120g) almond meal (ground almonds)

¾ cup (110g) coconut sugar

½ cup (75g) plain (all-purpose) wholemeal (whole-wheat) flour

1 teaspoon baking powder

1 teaspoon ground cinnamon

½ teaspoon ground ginger

1 cup (115g) roughly chopped pecans

¼ cup (40g) raisins

1½ cups (180g) peeled and grated carrot

1 egg

½ cup (125ml) light-flavoured extra virgin olive oil

cream cheese frosting

125g cream cheese, softened

1 teaspoon finely grated lemon rind

¼ cup (40g) icing (confectioner's) sugar, sifted

Preheat oven to 180°C (350°F).

Combine the oats, almond meal, sugar, flour, baking powder, cinnamon, ginger, pecans and raisins in a bowl.

Add the carrot, egg and oil and mix to combine.

Drop 12 x 2 heaped tablespoons of the cookie dough onto a large baking tray lined with non-stick baking paper and flatten slightly.

Bake for 25 minutes or until the cookies are golden. Allow to cool on the tray.

To make the cream cheese frosting, place the cream cheese, lemon rind and icing sugar into a food processor and process until smooth.

Sandwich the cookies together with the frosting before serving. **MAKES 6 SANDWICHES**

These cookies are amazing with or without the frosting—you choose.

This is my GO-TO TART for any occasion – from afternoon tea to after-dark. *Look no further* than the season's fruit bounty for the SWEETEST RESULTS.

any fruit tart

1½ cups (180g) plain (all-purpose) wholemeal (whole-wheat) spelt flour, plus extra for dusting

⅓ cup (75g) raw caster (superfine) sugar

125g very cold unsalted butter

¼ cup (60ml) ice-cold water

1 teaspoon vanilla extract

pure maple syrup or honey, to glaze

1 tablespoon demerara sugar

4 sprigs lemon thyme, to serve

vanilla bean yoghurt or ice-cream, to serve

almond filling

⅓ cup (45g) almond meal (ground almonds)

2 teaspoons finely grated lemon rind

⅓ cup (75g) raw caster (superfine) sugar

6 plums, stones removed and quartered[+]

1 cup (125g) fresh or frozen blueberries[+]

Place the flour and sugar in a bowl. Using a box grater, grate the butter into the flour. Add the water and vanilla, using your fingertips to combine until a soft dough forms. Shape into a disc.

Dust the pastry with extra flour and roll out between two sheets of non-stick baking paper until you have a rough 30cm (12 inch) round that is approximately 4mm (³⁄₁₆ inch) thick. Place onto a baking tray and refrigerate until firm. Remove the top sheet of baking paper.

Preheat oven to 180°C (350°F).

To make the almond filling, mix the almond meal, lemon rind and sugar together. Sprinkle over the pastry, leaving a 5cm (2 inch) border.

Top with the plums and blueberries. Fold the excess pastry over to form an edge.

Using a pastry brush, glaze the fruit with maple syrup or honey and sprinkle the pastry with demerara sugar. Bake for 40–45 minutes or until crisp and golden.

Serve the tart warm or cold with lemon thyme sprigs, vanilla bean yoghurt or ice-cream. **SERVES 8**

+ *Choose your own fruit combination. You could use either 8 apricots, 6 plums, 3 peaches, or 4 nectarines, halved and stones removed. You could also swap the blueberries for strawberries or blackberries.*

In the cooler months, try sliced apples or pears with frozen berries for a tangy pop of flavour.

SCAN THIS CODE FOR RECIPE VIDEO

These **OUTRAGEOUSLY GOOD** cookies hit all the high notes: crisp edges, *a fudgy centre*, and bursts of chocolate and macadamias to **SEAL THE DEAL**.

double choc macadamia cookies

1 cup (250g) cashew butter
150g dark (70% cocoa) chocolate, melted
1 cup (240g) firmly packed brown sugar
⅓ cup (80ml) light-flavoured extra virgin olive oil
¼ cup (60ml) milk or nut milk
2 tablespoons pure maple syrup
1 teaspoon vanilla extract
1 egg
1½ cups (180g) plain (all-purpose) wholemeal
  (whole-wheat) spelt flour
¼ teaspoon bicarbonate of (baking) soda
¼ teaspoon baking powder
100g chopped dark (70% cocoa) chocolate, extra
¾ cup (100g) macadamias, halved

Preheat oven to 180°C (350°F).

Place the cashew butter, melted chocolate, sugar, oil, milk, maple syrup, vanilla and egg in a large bowl and mix well to combine.

Mix the flour, bicarbonate of soda and baking powder together in a bowl to combine. Sift the flour mixture into the chocolate mixture and mix well. Add the chocolate and macadamias and fold through. Refrigerate the dough for 20 minutes or until firm.

Place 6 x ⅓ cupfuls of the mixture onto a large baking tray lined with non-stick baking paper. Bake for 14–16 minutes. Allow cookies to cool on the tray for 5 minutes, then cool on wire racks. Repeat with remaining mixture. **MAKES 12**

Macadamias can easily be swapped for halved pecans, walnuts or almonds.

This portable, TAKE-ANYWHERE PIE can travel safely to *picnics and dinner parties* in the tray it's baked in. JUST WRAP IT in a tea towel *and go!*

blackberry tray pie

1½ cups (210g) plain (all-purpose) wholemeal (whole-wheat) spelt flour
¾ cup (110g) plain (all purpose) flour
⅓ cup (75g) caster (superfine) sugar
185g very cold unsalted butter
⅓ cup (80ml) ice-cold water
2 teaspoons vanilla extract
vanilla bean yoghurt or ice-cream, to serve
blackberry filling
⅓ cup (45g) almond meal (ground almonds)
1 teaspoon finely grated lemon rind
⅓ cup (75g) caster (superfine) sugar, extra
1 tablespoon cornflour (cornstarch)
4¾ cups (600g) fresh or frozen blackberries

Place the flours and sugar in a bowl. Using a box grater, grate the butter into the flour.

Add the water and vanilla and use your fingertips to mix until the dough starts to clump together.

Press the pastry into a 20cm x 30cm (8 inch x 12 inch) baking tray lined with non-stick baking paper, making sure to press all the way up the sides. Refrigerate until firm.

Preheat oven to 180°C (350°F).

To make the blackberry filling, place the almond meal, lemon rind and 2 tablespoons sugar in a bowl and mix to combine. Sprinkle the almond mixture over the pastry. Place the remaining sugar, cornflour and blackberries in a bowl and toss to coat. Scatter the blackberries over the almond mixture.

Bake for 50–55 minutes or until the edges are golden. Serve the tart warm or cold with vanilla bean yoghurt or ice-cream. **SERVES 8**

Try this tart with any berry that catches your eye.

I love how these tray scones *come together* so easily.
I also love that they are loaded with BETTER-FOR-YOU
ingredients, making them the *perfect snack.*

blueberry, lemon and yoghurt scones

½ cup (75g) coconut sugar
⅓ cup (80ml) light-flavoured extra virgin olive oil
1¼ cups (350g) plain thick yoghurt
1 teaspoon vanilla extract
2 teaspoons finely grated lemon rind
1 cup (120g) plain (all-purpose) wholemeal
   (whole-wheat) spelt flour, plus extra for dusting
¾ cup (120g) buckwheat flour
½ cup (60g) almond meal (ground almonds)
2 tablespoons white chia seeds
3 teaspoons baking powder
2 cups (250g) frozen blueberries
demerara sugar, for sprinkling
store-bought creamed honey, to serve

Preheat oven to 180°C (350°F).

Place the coconut sugar, oil, yoghurt, vanilla and lemon rind into a bowl and whisk to combine.

In a separate bowl, mix the flours, almond meal, chia and baking powder together to combine.

Make a well in the centre, add the yoghurt mixture and use a butter knife or a flat spatula to gently mix the dough until almost combined[+]. Add the frozen blueberries and stir through.

Lay the dough out onto a large baking tray lined with non-stick baking paper.

Using lightly floured hands, bring the dough together and flatten out into a rough 20cm (8 inch) round.

Using a sharp knife, cut into 8 pieces and sprinkle the top with demerara sugar. Bake for 45 minutes or until golden-brown.

Serve with creamed honey, if you like. **SERVES 8**

+ *It is important to work quickly when using yoghurt and baking powder as these contain active ingredients.*

Get creative with these scones! Frozen raspberries, blackberries or chopped soft fresh dates will all shine.

Packed full of *all the good things*, this granola
is JUST TOO GOOD to reserve for breakfast.
It's the *perfect moreish*, crunchy ANYTIME SNACK.

cashew honey nut and seed granola

2 cups (180g) rolled oats
1 cup (100g) walnuts
⅓ cup (55g) pepitas (pumpkin seeds)
⅓ cup (55g) sunflower seeds
2 teaspoons ground cinnamon
½ cup (125g) cashew butter
½ cup (180g) honey
2 teaspoons vanilla extract
¼ cup (60ml) light-flavoured extra virgin olive oil
sliced fresh fruit, honey and vanilla bean yoghurt,
  to serve

Preheat oven to 160°C (325°F).

Place the oats, walnuts, pepitas, sunflower seeds and cinnamon into a bowl and mix to combine. In a small bowl, combine the cashew butter, honey, vanilla and oil. Pour into the dry ingredients and mix well.

Place onto a large baking tray lined with non-stick baking paper and bake for 18–20 minutes, turning halfway, or until the granola is golden and crisp.

Serve with fruit, honey and vanilla yoghurt. **MAKES 6 CUPS**

You can swap the cashew butter for almond butter or tahini.

chapter two
One Pan

An *all-purpose* heatproof frying pan is your new BEST FRIEND in the kitchen. It means you can flit from stovetop to oven in ONE EASY STEP and skip all the *in-between fuss*. You're rewarded with GOOEY CENTRES and *deeply bronzed* tops, whether it's a *bubbling, crisp-edged* lasagne or the perfect FLUFFY-CENTRED, golden-topped *one-pan skillet* cake. You're welcome!

This could be the EASIEST QUICHE *you'll ever make*. COOK THE PASTRY on the paper it's rolled on and fill with *delicious super-greens* and cheese.

pan kale and feta quiche

1¾ cups (210g) plain (all-purpose) wholemeal
   (whole-wheat) spelt flour, plus extra for dusting
⅓ cup (25g) finely grated parmesan
½ cup (140g) plain thick yoghurt
⅓ cup (80ml) extra virgin olive oil
quiche filling
5½ cups (190g) firmly packed shredded kale leaves
1½ cups (360g) fresh ricotta
8 eggs
½ cup (125ml) milk
½ cup (40g) finely grated parmesan
½ cup (26g) chopped flat-leaf (Italian) parsley leaves
¼ cup (12g) chopped dill leaves
sea salt and cracked black pepper
150g feta, broken into large chunks

Preheat oven to 180°C (350°F).

To make the pastry, place the flour, parmesan, yoghurt and oil into a bowl and mix to combine. Roll the dough out between two sheets of non-stick baking paper until 2–3 mm (1/16–1/8 inch) thick. Loosen the pastry on the paper so it's not stuck to it, then discard the top sheet.

Place the pastry and paper into a deep 22cm (8½ inch) ovenproof frying pan, allowing the paper to overhang the pan. Bake for 15 minutes or until lightly golden.

While the pastry is cooking, make the filling. Place the kale into a bowl and cover with boiling water. Allow to stand for 2 minutes, then drain. Place kale between absorbent kitchen paper and squeeze out any excess moisture.

Place ricotta, eggs, milk and parmesan into a bowl and whisk to combine. Add the kale, parsley, dill, salt and pepper and mix to combine.

Pour into the baked pastry shell, top with the feta and bake for 35–40 minutes or until just set. **SERVES 4**

You can switch up parsley or dill for mint, and kale for silverbeet or rainbow chard leaves.

SCAN THIS CODE FOR RECIPE VIDEO

A baked ALL-IN-ONE curry that is big on *spiced-up flavour* and goodness and light on effort. WHERE DO WE SIGN UP?

baked red curry chicken and coconut dhal

2 tablespoons extra virgin olive oil
2 onions, sliced
2 tablespoons finely grated ginger
1 long red chilli, sliced
½ teaspoon ground cumin
½ teaspoon ground coriander (cilantro)
1 teaspoon ground turmeric
2 cups (500ml) good-quality chicken stock
1 x 400ml can coconut milk
½ cup (125ml) water
2 cups (400g) split red lentils
6 stalks kale (170g), stems removed and leaves
   roughly chopped
sea salt and cracked black pepper
coriander (cilantro) leaves and lime wedges, to serve
red curry chicken
¼ cup (75g) red curry paste
½ cup (125ml) thick coconut cream
6 x 145g small chicken thighs on the bone, skin-on[+]

Preheat oven to 220°C (425°F).

To make the red curry chicken, mix the curry paste and coconut cream together and spread over the skin of the chicken. Set aside.

Heat a large, deep, round ovenproof frying pan over medium-high heat. Add the oil and onions and cook, stirring occasionally for 7 minutes, or until golden. Add the ginger, chilli, cumin, coriander and turmeric and cook for 1 minute.

Add the stock, coconut milk, water and lentils to the pan and bring to a simmer. Fold the kale through and sprinkle with salt and pepper.

Arrange the chicken over the lentils and place the pan into the oven. Bake uncovered for 40 minutes or until the chicken is golden and cooked through. Top with coriander and serve with lime wedges. **SERVES 6**
+ *You can remove the skin from the chicken if you prefer.*

The coconut dhal and kale make this one-pan chicken a complete meal on its own!

Porcini mushrooms give these meatballs a *deliciously earthy* SAVOURY KICK. Just the SHAKE-UP your midweek repertoire needed.

porcini meatballs with white beans and mozzarella

35g dried porcini mushrooms, sliced

1 cup (250ml) hot good-quality beef or vegetable stock

650g beef or plant-based mince

1 clove garlic, crushed

2 tablespoons oregano leaves, roughly chopped,
  plus 4 sprigs, extra

sea salt and cracked black pepper

2 tablespoons extra virgin olive oil

2 x 400g cans white (cannellini) beans,
  rinsed and drained

10 stalks (200g) cavolo nero (Tuscan kale),
  stems removed

200g fresh mozzarella, drained and sliced

⅓ cup (25g) finely grated parmesan

spaghetti or crusty bread, to serve

Soak the porcini in hot beef stock for 20 minutes. Drain well, reserving the hot beef stock. Set aside.

Finely chop the porcini and mix with the mince, garlic, oregano, salt and pepper to combine. Roll ¼ cupfuls of the mixture into balls.

Heat a large 22cm (8½ inch) ovenproof frying pan over medium-high heat. Add oil and meatballs and cook for 3 minutes each side or until browned all over. Remove meatballs from the pan and set aside.

Add white beans and reserved stock to the pan and simmer for 5 minutes or until the stock has reduced by half. Return meatballs to the pan and cook for 2 minutes. Add the cavolo nero and cook for 1 minute.

Preheat oven grill (broiler) to high. Top the meatballs with mozzarella, parmesan and oregano sprigs and grill for 7–8 minutes or until golden.

Serve with spaghetti or slices of crusty bread. SERVES 4

These make the ultimate cheesy meatball sandwich!

Bring the cafe home with this CRISP AND GOLDEN *potato cake* crowned with a Scandi-inspired mix of SMOKY, HERBY, CREAMY things.

crispy potato cake with lemon yoghurt and smoked trout

750g starchy potatoes, peeled
1 onion, peeled
2 tablespoons white chia seeds
2 eggs
¼ cup (5g) small dill sprigs
2 teaspoons chopped rosemary leaves
sea salt and cracked black pepper
¼ cup (60ml) extra virgin olive oil, plus extra
   for brushing
2 cups (50g) rocket (arugula) leaves
300g smoked ocean trout
lemon wedges, to serve
lemon yoghurt
1 cup (280g) plain thick yoghurt
rind of 1 lemon
1 tablespoon small dill sprigs, plus extra to serve
1 tablespoon capers, plus extra to serve

Preheat oven to 220°C (425°F).

Coarsely grate the potatoes and onion and press between absorbent kitchen paper to remove any excess moisture. Place the mixture in a bowl with the chia, eggs, dill, rosemary, salt and pepper and mix to combine.

Heat a 20cm (8 inch) ovenproof non-stick frying pan over medium-high heat. Add the oil and heat for 30 seconds. Add the potato mixture and flatten with a spatula. Cook for 2 minutes, then brush the top of the potato cake with extra oil.

Place the pan into the oven and bake for 15 minutes or until the bottom is brown and the edges are crisp. Turn the oven to grill (broiler) and grill the potato cake for 5 minutes or until the top is golden-brown.

To make the lemon yoghurt, place the yoghurt, lemon rind, dill and capers into a bowl and mix to combine.

To serve, top the potato cake with the lemon yoghurt, rocket, trout, extra dill and capers, and lemon wedges.

SERVES 4

Smoked salmon works just as well as smoked trout.

A few clever BIG-HITTING ingredients lift these *Middle Eastern-inspired* koftas to SUPER-TASTY, SUPER-CHARGED new heights.

lamb koftas with tomato and pomegranate salad

600g lamb or plant-based mince
1½ cups (210g) cooked quinoa
¼ cup (20g) psyllium husks
¼ cup (14g) chopped mint leaves
¼ cup (6g) flat-leaf (Italian) parsley leaves
1 tablespoon pomegranate molasses
sea salt and cracked black pepper
150g feta, broken into large chunks
2 tablespoons extra virgin olive oil
store-bought hummus and flatbread, to serve
tomato and pomegranate salad
2 tablespoons pomegranate molasses
¼ cup (60ml) extra virgin olive oil
250g cherry tomatoes, halved
5 cups (140g) rocket (arugula) leaves
½ cup (90g) pomegranate seeds
1 cup (16g) mint leaves
1 cup (24g) flat-leaf (Italian) parsley leaves

To make the lamb koftas, place the mince, quinoa, psyllium, mint, parsley, pomegranate molasses, salt and pepper in a bowl and mix to combine. Add the feta and gently fold through. Roll ¼ cupfuls of the mixture into balls and flatten slightly.

Heat a large non-stick frying pan over medium heat. Add oil and cook koftas in batches for 4–5 minutes each side, or until browned and cooked through.

To make the tomato and pomegranate salad, mix the pomegranate molasses and oil in a small bowl to combine. Place the tomatoes, rocket, pomegranate seeds, mint and parsley in a bowl and toss together. Add the dressing and toss to coat.

Serve the koftas with the salad, hummus and flatbread.
SERVES 4

If you can't find pomegranate molasses, try balsamic vinegar instead.

These are baked eggs taken to a new **LEVEL OF YUM.**
Kimchi *brings the party* to this brunch-time favourite
thanks to its brightness and **RICH FLAVOUR.**

spicy kimchi eggs

2 tablespoons extra virgin olive oil
2 onions, finely sliced
1½ cups (420g) kimchi, chopped
2 x 400g cans cherry tomatoes
3 cups (75g) baby spinach leaves
4 eggs
black sesame seeds, sliced green onion (scallions)
  and toasted sourdough, to serve

Heat a large frying pan over medium-high heat. Add the
oil and onions and cook for 7 minutes or until just golden.

Add the kimchi and tomatoes, reduce heat to low, and
simmer for 8–10 minutes or until thickened slightly. Stir
the spinach through and cook for 1 minute.

Reduce heat to low. Make 4 indents in the kimchi and
greens mixture and break an egg into each one. Cover
with a lid and cook for 4–5 minutes or until the eggs are
cooked to your liking.

Sprinkle with black sesame seeds and green onion
and serve with toasted sourdough. **SERVES 2-4**

Use shredded kale or cavolo nero leaves instead of spinach, if you prefer.

These *moreish meatballs* are coated in a PUNCHY SWEET (but not-too-sweet) and *spicy sauce* that takes them from ZERO TO A HUNDRED in minutes.

spiced meatballs in sticky chilli sauce

500g beef or plant-based mince

1 clove garlic, crushed

1 tablespoon gochujang (Korean chilli paste)[+]
   or mild chilli paste

3 green onions (scallions), finely chopped

1 tablespoon finely grated ginger

1 teaspoon sesame oil

1 tablespoon vegetable oil

cooked brown basmati rice, kimchi, sliced cucumber,
   thinly sliced chillies and sesame seeds, to serve

sticky chilli sauce

2 tablespoons soy sauce

2 tablespoons honey

2 tablespoons rice wine vinegar

1 tablespoon gochujang (Korean chilli paste)
   or mild chilli paste

1 tablespoon finely grated ginger

2 cloves garlic, finely grated

To make the sticky chilli sauce, place the soy sauce, honey, rice wine vinegar, gochujang, ginger and garlic in a bowl and mix to combine. Set aside.

To make the meatballs, place the mince, garlic, gochujang, green onion, ginger and sesame oil in a bowl and mix to combine. Roll tablespoons of the mixture into balls.

Heat a non-stick frying pan over medium heat. Add the vegetable oil and cook the meatballs for 5 minutes or until browned. Add the sticky chilli sauce and cook for 5 minutes, stirring gently to coat the meatballs.

Serve the meatballs with rice, kimchi and cucumber, and top with chilli and sesame seeds. SERVES 4

+ *You can find gochujang in supermarkets, Asian grocers and gourmet food stores. You could also use any mild chilli paste instead.*

Switch up regular rice for cauliflower rice for a lighter alternative.

Take EVERYTHING YOU LOVE about lasagne – *golden, bubbling top,* crisp edges, GOOEY CENTRE – and refresh with NOURISHING GREENS for this lighter take.

zucchini, spinach and mozzarella lasagne

850g English spinach (about 4 bunches), stems removed
4 cups (1kg) fresh ricotta
1 cup (80g) finely grated parmesan, plus extra
1 cup (56g) chopped mint leaves
1 cup (52g) chopped flat-leaf (Italian) parsley leaves
sea salt and cracked black pepper
3 x 30cm (12 inch) or 6 x 15cm (6 inch) square fresh lasagne sheets, blanched
4 zucchini (courgette), thinly sliced using a mandoline
3 x 100g fresh mozzarella, drained and sliced
extra virgin olive oil, for brushing

Preheat oven to 200°C (400°F).

Place the spinach into a large heatproof bowl and cover with boiling water. Allow to stand for 10 seconds, then drain. Press the spinach between absorbent kitchen paper to remove any excess moisture.

Roughly chop the spinach and place into a bowl with the ricotta, parmesan, mint, parsley, salt and pepper, and mix to combine.

To assemble the lasagne, place 1 lasagne sheet into the base of a lightly greased 22cm (8½ inch) ovenproof frying pan. Top with 1½ cupfuls of the spinach and ricotta mixture, a layer of zucchini, and then a layer of mozzarella. Repeat layering with remaining lasagne sheets, spinach and ricotta mixture, zucchini, and mozzarella, finishing with zucchini.

Brush the zucchini with oil, sprinkle with extra parmesan and bake for 1 hour or until golden-brown.
SERVES 4–6

Every fresh ricotta is different so if your ricotta mixture is a little dry, add a tablespoon of milk.

Fluffy in the centre and BRONZED ON TOP
with *bursts of vine-ripened tomatoes*, this frittata
is TOO GOOD to limit to just sunrise.

all day breakfast frittata

2 tablespoons extra virgin olive oil
1 leek, finely sliced
400g vine-ripened cherry tomatoes
8 stalks (160g) cavolo nero (Tuscan kale),
stems removed
8 eggs
1 cup (250ml) milk
1 tablespoon wholegrain mustard
sea salt and cracked black pepper
1 cup (240g) fresh ricotta
basil leaves, prosciutto, and toasted sourdough,
to serve

Preheat oven to 220°C (425°F).

Place the oil, leek and cherry tomatoes into a large 22cm (8½ inch) ovenproof frying pan and toss to coat. Bake for 10–15 minutes or until the tomatoes are slightly blistered. Remove pan from the oven and remove tomatoes from the pan. Set aside. Add the cavolo nero to the hot pan and stir until soft.

Reduce oven temperature to 180°C (350°F).

Whisk together the eggs, milk, mustard, salt and pepper. Pour into the pan and stir gently to distribute the eggs and cavolo nero evenly. Add spoonfuls of ricotta over the frittata and top with the tomatoes.

Bake in the oven for 20–25 minutes or until almost set. Stand for 5 minutes.

Serve frittata with basil, prosciutto and toasted sourdough. **SERVES 4**

Swap prosciutto for avocado or your favourite egg accompaniments.

This BETTER-FOR-YOU spin on the *Tex-Mex favourite* is a great way to *make the most* of that leftover cooked chicken. The perfect combo of *smoky-gooey-yum.*

chipotle and kale quesadillas

6 cups (210g) firmly packed shredded kale leaves

2 cups (320g) cooked shredded chicken or
  chopped firm tofu

½ cup (120g) chipotle chillies in adobo sauce,
  chillies finely chopped and sauce reserved

400g fresh mozzarella, grated

1 red onion, finely sliced

2 teaspoons sweet smoked paprika

sea salt and cracked black pepper

8 x 20cm (8 inch) wholegrain (whole-wheat)
  flour tortillas

extra virgin olive oil, to brush

avocado and lime wedges, to serve

Place the kale in a bowl and cover with boiling water. Allow to stand for 2 minutes, then drain. Place the kale between absorbent kitchen paper and press firmly to remove excess moisture.

Place the kale, chicken, chipotle chillies and sauce, half the mozzarella, red onion, paprika, salt and pepper in a bowl and mix to combine.

Place the tortillas on a clean work surface and brush one side with oil. Turn four of the tortillas over so that they are oil-side down and top with the kale and chicken mixture. Sprinkle with the remaining mozzarella and top with the remaining tortillas.

Heat a large non-stick frying pan over medium heat. Place 1 quesadilla into the pan, place a large heatproof plate on top of it and weigh it down with something heavy, like two cans of food[+]. Cook the quesadilla for 4–5 minutes each side or until golden and the cheese has melted. Repeat with remaining quesadillas.

Slice each quesadilla and serve with avocado and lime.

SERVES 4

+ *The plate and cans allow the tortilla to cook evenly.*

You could also serve these quesadillas with a lime mayonnaise or aioli.

This ONE-PAN baked feta is the *perfect cheesy blanket* for pasta or GOOEY DIP for crusty bread. I LOVE the *pops of sweet tomato* throughout it.

pan-baked tomato and parmesan feta

¼ cup (60ml) extra virgin olive oil
2 red onions, sliced
3 cloves garlic, sliced
12 stalks cavolo nero (about 240g), stems removed
3 x 400g cans cherry tomatoes
sea salt and cracked black pepper
⅓ cup (25g) finely grated parmesan
6 sprigs lemon thyme
2 x 200g feta pieces
basil leaves, to serve
pasta or toasted sourdough, to serve

Heat a large ovenproof frying pan over medium heat.

Add 1 tablespoon oil and onions and cook for 8 minutes or until the onions are lightly golden. Add the garlic and cook for 2 minutes.

Add the cavolo nero and cook for 1 minute or until wilted. Add the tomatoes, salt and pepper and stir to combine. Bring to the boil. Reduce heat to low and simmer for 15 minutes, stirring occasionally until the tomato sauce thickens slightly. Remove from the heat.

Preheat oven grill (broiler) to high.

Meanwhile, place the parmesan, thyme and remaining oil in a bowl and mix to combine.

Place the feta in the centre of the pan and top with the parmesan mixture.

Grill for 8–10 minutes or until the parmesan is golden. Serve with fresh basil leaves and pasta or thick slices of toasted sourdough. **SERVES 4**

This one-pan pasta sauce is finished in the oven for that gooey factor!

SLIPPERY, CHEWY udon glistening under a *sticky honey* soy sauce, laced with CRUNCHY GREENS... these *better-than-take-out* noodles speak for themselves.

honey soy tofu with udon noodles

600g firm tofu, cut into cubes
2 tablespoons vegetable oil
800g fresh udon noodles, rinsed
1 bunch gai lan (Chinese broccoli), trimmed and
   halved lengthways
250g snow peas (mange tout), halved lengthways
chilli paste and coriander (cilantro) leaves, to serve
honey soy marinade
½ cup (180g) honey
⅓ cup (80ml) black vinegar
¼ cup (60ml) soy sauce
4 cloves garlic, finely grated

To make the honey soy marinade, mix the honey, black vinegar, soy sauce and garlic in a bowl to combine. Place the tofu and half the marinade in a bowl and mix to coat.

Heat a large frying pan or wok over medium-high heat. Add the oil and marinated tofu and cook for 2–3 minutes or until the tofu starts to colour. Add the noodles and remaining marinade and cook for 8–10 minutes, stirring occasionally, until the noodles are golden and the sauce thickens. Add the gai lan and snow peas and cook for 2 minutes or until the greens are just tender.

To serve, divide noodles between bowls and top with the chilli paste and coriander. **SERVES 4**

Swap the tofu for sliced chicken breast or peeled and cleaned raw king prawns.

Who doesn't love a burger night! These *veg-forward* buns are BURSTING WITH GOODNESS and will *still* *satisfy* those COMFORT FOOD cravings.

pumpkin tofu burgers with herb mayonnaise

380g firm tofu

2 cups (300g) firmly packed grated pumpkin

⅔ cup (180g) hulled tahini

¼ cup (13g) chopped flat-leaf (Italian) parsley leaves

2 tablespoons nutritional yeast

2 tablespoons extra virgin olive oil

sea salt and cracked black pepper

4 burger buns, halved

1 cup (150g) firmly packed grated beetroot

1 cup (150g) firmly packed grated carrot

½ cup (150g) caramelised onion relish

8 butter lettuce leaves

pickles, to serve

herb mayonnaise

¾ cup (225g) whole egg mayonnaise

2 tablespoons chopped basil leaves

½ teaspoon finely grated garlic

Preheat oven to 180°C (350°F)

Place the tofu between absorbent kitchen paper and press firmly to release any excess moisture.

Using your fingertips, crumble the tofu into small pieces into a bowl. Add the pumpkin, tahini, parsley, nutritional yeast, salt and pepper and mix to combine.

Heat a large ovenproof non-stick frying pan over medium heat. Divide the pumpkin and tofu mixture into 4 large flat patties. Add the oil and cook the patties for 8 minutes each side or until golden and crisp. Transfer pan to the oven and bake the patties for 15 minutes.

To make the herb mayonnaise, mix the mayonnaise, basil and garlic in a bowl to combine.

Spread each bun base with herb mayonnaise and divide the beetroot, carrot, caramelised onion, lettuce, and pumpkin tofu patties between bun bases. Sandwich with the bun tops and serve with pickles. SERVES 4

Turn up the heat with some store-bought chilli sauce, if you like.

With their *juicy filling* and CRISPY LATTICE CRUST that forms as the water evaporates and the *pastry browns*, these POT STICKERS will have you hooked.

ginger chicken pot sticker dumplings

200g chicken mince
2 green onions (scallions), finely sliced
1 tablespoon finely grated ginger
2 tablespoons hoisin sauce
16 store-bought gow gee wrappers
2 teaspoons cornflour (cornstarch)
¾ cup (180ml) water, plus extra
1 tablespoon vegetable oil
thinly sliced green onions (scallions), baby shiso leaves
   or mint leaves, blanched bok choy and sesame seeds,
   to serve
vinegar ginger dipping sauce
2 teaspoons finely grated ginger
1 teaspoon chilli paste
2 teaspoons soy sauce
⅓ cup (80ml) black vinegar

To make the vinegar ginger dipping sauce, combine the ginger, chilli paste, soy and black vinegar and set aside.

To make the dumplings, place the chicken, green onions, ginger and hoisin in a bowl and mix well to combine.

Arrange the gow gee wrappers on a clean work surface.

Place 1 teaspoon of the chicken mixture in the centre of each wrapper. Brush the edge of the wrapper with a little water, fold to enclose and pinch to seal. Repeat with remaining wrappers and filling.

Whisk the cornflour and water together in a small bowl to combine.

Heat the oil in a 24cm (9½ inch) non-stick frying pan over medium heat. Add the dumplings, flat-side down, and cook for 2 minutes. Pour the cornflour mixture over the top, cover with a tight-fitting lid and cook for a further 5 minutes. Remove lid and cook for 4–5 minutes or until the water has evaporated, leaving a golden lattice.

Invert dumplings onto a plate and serve with the vinegar ginger dipping sauce, green onion, baby shiso leaves, bok choy and sesame seeds, if you like. **SERVES 2**

Change up the filling by swapping the chicken for pork mince or finely chopped raw prawn meat.

Eggs take CENTRE STAGE in this *fun one-pan* dish.
It's LOADED WITH COLOUR, flavour and goodness
and makes a *tasty breakfast*, lunch or dinner.

chilli egg cups

12 stalks (about 2 bunches) gai lan (Chinese broccoli)

3 green onions (scallions), trimmed and quartered,
    plus extra, sliced

vegetable oil, for brushing

6 large eggs

4 cups (660g) cooked brown rice, to serve

sliced chilli, coriander (cilantro) leaves and soy sauce,
    to serve

chilli ginger oil

2 cloves garlic, finely grated

1 long red chilli, finely chopped

3 teaspoons finely grated ginger

⅓ cup (80ml) light-flavoured extra virgin olive oil

1 teaspoon sesame oil

Preheat oven to 220°C (425°F).

Place the gai lan and quartered green onions in a
heatproof bowl and cover with boiling water. Allow to
stand for 30 seconds or until the gai lan stems have
softened. Drain and pat dry with absorbent kitchen paper.

Arrange 2 stalks gai lan around the edge of each hole in
a lightly-greased 6 x 1-cup-capacity (250ml) muffin tin[+].
Sprinkle with the extra green onions.

To make the chilli ginger oil, mix the garlic, chilli, ginger
and oils in a bowl to combine. Reserve a quarter of the
oil mixture and set aside.

Spoon the remaining chilli ginger oil over the greens
in the tin. Add an egg to the centre of each greens-lined
hole and drizzle with the remaining chilli oil. Bake for
8–12 minutes or until cooked.

Divide egg cups between plates and serve with cooked
brown rice, sliced chilli, coriander leaves and soy sauce.

SERVES 3–4

+ *If the gai lan is too firm to bend, simply halve the stems
to make them easier to shape.*

*Serve these egg cups
for breakfast with
prosciutto and sourdough
instead of rice.*

If the classic mince and *eggplant parmigiana* is a cosy winter jacket, consider this SUPER-TASTY VERSION a light, *bright summer sweater.*

summer eggplant parmigiana

24 x 1½ cm (⅝ inch) thick slices (about 3 large)
    eggplant (aubergine)
extra virgin olive oil, for brushing
sea salt flakes, for sprinkling
2 tablespoons extra virgin olive oil, plus extra
    for drizzling
1 large onion, thinly sliced
4 cloves garlic, thinly sliced
⅓ cup (80ml) dry white wine
800g cherry tomatoes, halved
½ cup (125ml) good-quality chicken or vegetable stock
sea salt and cracked black pepper
½ cup (10g) basil leaves, plus extra to serve
ricotta parmesan filling
2 cups (480g) fresh ricotta
½ cup (40g) finely grated parmesan
2 tablespoons shredded basil leaves
sea salt and cracked black pepper
parmesan crumb
½ cup (40g) finely grated parmesan
½ cup (35g) fresh breadcrumbs
2 tablespoons oregano leaves

Preheat oven to 220°C (425°F).

To make the parmesan crumb, combine the parmesan, breadcrumbs and oregano. Set aside.

Brush each side of the eggplant with oil and sprinkle with salt.

Heat a large ovenproof frying pan over medium-high heat. Cook the eggplant in batches for 1 minute each side or until golden. Remove from the pan and set aside. Wipe the pan clean.

Add the oil and onion to the pan and cook for 5–6 minutes or until golden. Add the garlic and cook for 1–2 minutes. Add the wine and simmer for 2 minutes.

Add the cherry tomatoes, stock, salt and pepper and bring to a simmer, stirring occasionally for 15–20 minutes or until the sauce has thickened. Stir the basil through.

To make the ricotta parmesan filling, mix the ricotta, parmesan, basil, salt and pepper together to combine.

Place 12 eggplant slices on a clean work surface and top each slice with a heaped tablespoon of the ricotta parmesan filling. Top with the remaining eggplant slices.

Place the eggplant sandwiches on top of the tomato sauce. Sprinkle each eggplant with the parmesan crumb and drizzle with oil.

Bake for 30–35 minutes or until the eggplant is soft and the crumb is golden. Serve with extra basil leaves.
SERVES 4

The crunchy parmesan crumb is a great textural contrast to the tender eggplant.

One Pan

sweet

Forget *searching the cupboards* for the RIGHT CAKE TIN. Your humble frying pan or skillet works *double time* here to create the perfect ONE-PAN CAKE.

fruit-topped skillet cake

125g unsalted butter

½ cup (125ml) milk

2 teaspoons vanilla extract

¾ cup (165g) raw caster (superfine) sugar, plus extra

1 cup (80g) desiccated coconut

1½ cups (225g) wholemeal (whole-wheat) self-raising (self-rising) flour

1 teaspoon baking powder

3 eggs

3 stone fruits of your choice, stones removed and sliced into wedges[+]

1½ cups (185g) fresh or frozen raspberries[+]

vanilla bean yoghurt or ice-cream, to serve

Preheat oven to 160°C (325°F).

Place the butter, milk and vanilla into a 22cm (8½ inch) ovenproof frying pan. Stir over low heat until the butter has melted, then remove from the heat.

Add the caster sugar and coconut and mix to combine. Add the flour and baking powder and mix until smooth. Add the eggs and mix to combine.

Top the cake mix with the fruit and berries and sprinkle with extra sugar. Bake in the oven for 50 minutes or until cooked when tested with a skewer.

Serve cake warm with vanilla bean yoghurt or ice-cream.

SERVES 10

+ *You can switch up the fruit and berries with so many different combinations. Try 2 small apples sliced into wedges, or 2 small pears sliced into wedges. Blueberries and blackberries work well, too.*

To serve, scoop this cake into bowls like you would a pudding.

SCAN THIS CODE FOR RECIPE VIDEO

The SCENTS WAFTING from this cake as it bakes are incredible! It's so *light and airy* on the inside, with a DELICIOUSLY SYRUPY exterior.

earl grey tea and lemon cake

2 tablespoons Earl Grey loose leaf tea
1 cup (250ml) milk
2½ cups (375g) self-raising (self-rising) flour
1 cup (220g) raw caster (superfine) sugar
½ cup (75g) coconut sugar
4 eggs
125g unsalted butter, melted
1 cup (280g) plain thick yoghurt
2 teaspoons vanilla extract
1 teaspoon finely grated lemon rind
1 teaspoon finely grated orange rind
edible flowers, to serve (optional)
honey glaze
½ cup (125ml) strong brewed Earl Grey tea
¼ cup (90g) honey
¼ cup (60ml) lemon juice
¼ cup (60ml) orange juice

Preheat oven to 180°C (350°F).

Place the tea leaves and milk in a small saucepan over medium heat. Bring to a gentle simmer, then remove from the heat and allow to stand for 5 minutes. Strain and reserve the milk and discard the tea leaves.

Place the flour, sugars, eggs, butter, yoghurt, vanilla, lemon and orange rinds and the tea-infused milk into a large bowl and whisk until smooth. Pour into a greased 3-litre (12-cup) capacity bundt tin and bake for 30–35 minutes or until cooked when tested with a skewer. Place the tin onto a wire rack and allow cake to cool in the tin for 10 minutes. Gently remove the cake from the tin.

To make the honey glaze, place the brewed Earl Grey tea, honey, lemon and orange juice into a frying pan and simmer over medium heat for 10 minutes or until thickened and syrupy.

Pour the glaze over the cake before serving and top with edible flowers, if you like. SERVES 10–12

Brush the bundt tin with a little softened butter to ensure the cake releases easily.

In my house, muffins are a staple PORTABLE SNACK.
This *better-for-you*, fluffy-centred, *crunchy-topped*
version will be on HIGH ROTATION at your place.

raspberry yoghurt muffins with yoghurt drizzle

2 cups (240g) plain (all-purpose) wholemeal
(whole-wheat) spelt flour
¾ cup (90g) almond meal (ground almonds)
¾ cup (165g) raw caster (superfine) sugar
3 teaspoons baking powder
1⅓ cups (375g) plain thick yoghurt
2 teaspoons vanilla extract
1 egg
½ cup (125ml) light-flavoured extra virgin olive oil
3 cups (375g) frozen raspberries
yoghurt drizzle
⅓ cup (95g) plain thick yoghurt
3 teaspoons honey

Preheat oven to 180°C (350°F).

Place the spelt flour, almond meal, sugar and baking powder in a bowl and mix to combine. Make a well in the centre of the dry ingredients and add the yoghurt, vanilla, egg and oil and mix until just combined.

Add the raspberries and gently fold through until just combined.

Divide the mixture between 12 x ½ cup-capacity (125ml) muffin tins that have been greased or lined with paper cases and bake for 30–35 minutes or until cooked when tested with a skewer. Transfer to a wire rack to cool.

To make the yoghurt drizzle, place the yoghurt and honey in a bowl and whisk to combine.

Serve the muffins warm or at room temperature with the yoghurt drizzle. **MAKES 12**

These muffins are also delicious with blueberries, mixed berries or blackberries instead of raspberries.

SCAN THIS CODE FOR RECIPE VIDEO

Cook the oranges in the same pan you bake the cake in – easy! YOU'LL JUST LOVE the *delicious maple-orange crown* and NICE-FOR-YOU ingredients.

orange chia seed upside-down skillet cake

2 eggs
¾ cup (180ml) light-flavoured extra virgin olive oil
1 cup (280g) plain thick yoghurt
1 tablespoon finely grated orange rind
¾ cup (165g) raw caster (superfine) sugar
1 cup (80g) desiccated coconut
1¾ cups (280g) plain (all-purpose) white spelt flour
   or gluten-free plain (all-purpose) flour
¼ cup (50g) black chia seeds
3 teaspoons baking powder
orange topping
3 oranges, peeled and sliced in 1cm (½ inch) rounds
½ cup (125ml) pure maple syrup, plus extra to serve

Preheat oven to 160°C (325°F).

To make the topping, place the orange slices and maple syrup into a large 22cm (8½ inch) ovenproof frying pan over medium heat and cook for 25 minutes, or until the oranges begin to turn translucent. Remove pan from the heat.

To make the cake, place the eggs, oil, yoghurt, orange rind and sugar into a large bowl and whisk to combine. Add the coconut, flour, chia and baking powder and whisk to combine.

Carefully spoon the mixture over the top of the oranges and bake for 40 minutes or until cooked when tested with a skewer. Allow cake to cool in the pan for 10 minutes, then invert onto a serving plate.

Serve warm with extra maple syrup. **SERVES 10**

Orange slices perform a double act of retaining moisture and perfuming the entire cake.

SCAN THIS CODE FOR RECIPE VIDEO O

Pancakes are often flung into the '*breakfast treat*' basket, but my SUPER-YUM, nutritionally-upscaled stack is the *perfect morning fuel*.

complete breakfast pancakes

1 cup (160g) buckwheat flour
1 cup (120g) almond meal (ground almonds)
2 tablespoons hemp seeds
2 tablespoons flaxseed meal
1 teaspoon ground cinnamon
2½ teaspoons baking powder
½ cup (75g) coconut sugar
1 cup (260g) mashed banana (about 3 bananas)
¼ cup (60ml) light-flavoured extra virgin olive oil,
    plus extra for brushing
1¼ cups (310ml) milk or nut milk
plain or vanilla bean yoghurt, to serve
fresh fruit, to serve

Place the flour, almond meal, hemp seeds, flaxseed meal, cinnamon, baking powder and sugar into a large bowl and whisk to combine. Make a well in the centre, add the banana, oil and milk and whisk to combine.

Heat a large non-stick frying pan over medium heat and brush the pan with oil. In batches, cook ½-cupfuls (125ml) of the mixture for 3–4 minutes each side or until puffed and golden. Remove from the pan and keep warm.

Serve the pancakes with plain or vanilla bean yoghurt and fresh fruit. **MAKES 8**

These powerhouse pancakes will keep you going all morning!

THE BEAUTY of these scrolls is that *all the magic happens* in your HUMBLE FRYING PAN. Plus, the yoghurt keeps them super *moist and fluffy.*

raspberry yoghurt scrolls

2 cups (300g) self-raising (self-rising) flour

1½ cups (225g) wholemeal (whole-wheat) self-raising (self-rising) flour

⅓ cup (75g) raw caster (superfine) sugar

1½ teaspoons baking powder

3 teaspoons vanilla extract

1½ cups (420g) plain thick yoghurt

½ cup (125ml) light-flavoured extra virgin olive oil

pure maple syrup, for brushing

filling

2 cups (250g) frozen raspberries

2 tablespoons raw caster (superfine) sugar, extra

Preheat oven 180°C (350°F).

Place the flours, sugar and baking powder into a bowl and mix to combine. Place the vanilla, yoghurt and oil into a bowl and mix to combine. Make a well in the centre of the dry ingredients. Pour the yoghurt mixture in and mix with a butter knife until you have a rough dough.

Roll the dough out between two sheets of baking paper to form a 20cm x 35cm (8 inch x 13¾ inch) rectangle.

Remove the top layer of baking paper. Sprinkle the dough with frozen raspberries and the extra sugar. Working from the long edge, roll the dough over tightly to enclose the berries and then slice into 9 equal pieces.

Place scrolls into a 23cm (9 inch) ovenproof frying pan or 23cm (9 inch) cake tin lined with non-stick baking paper. Bake for 40–45 minutes or until golden. Brush with maple syrup while hot and serve. SERVES 9

Once you master these scrolls, you can get creative with so many different filling combinations! From apple and cinnamon, to blueberries tossed in elderflower cordial.

SCAN THIS CODE FOR RECIPE VIDEO

Few things can beat WARM, STICKY APPLES encased in *flaky pastry*. Serve this NOSTALGIA-TINGED dessert with a *scoop of your favourite* vanilla ice-cream.

caramelised apple skillet pie

¼ cup (55g) raw caster (superfine) sugar
6 red apples, thinly sliced
1 tablespoon lemon juice
1 teaspoon vanilla extract
pie crust
½ cup (125ml) light-flavoured extra virgin olive oil,
    for brushing
½ cup (110g) raw caster (superfine) sugar, extra
20 sheets filo pastry+

Heat a 20cm (8 inch) non-stick ovenproof frying pan over high heat. Sprinkle the sugar into the pan to coat it and once it starts to melt in places, add the apples. Allow apples to cook for 2 minutes, then add the lemon juice and vanilla and stir to combine. Cook the apples for a further 1–2 minutes or until they start to soften.

Remove apples from the pan with a slotted spoon and set aside in a heatproof bowl. Reduce pan juices until syrupy and pour over apples. Wash and dry the pan.

Preheat oven to 180°C (350°F).

To make the pie crust, brush the pan with oil and sprinkle with 1–2 tablespoons of the extra sugar to coat.

Lay filo pastry on a clean tea towel. Transfer one sheet of pastry onto a clean chopping board, brush with oil and sprinkle with more sugar. Repeat until 10 pastry sheets are used, then set stack aside and cover with a clean damp tea towel. Repeat process with remaining pastry.

Lay one stack of pastry in the pan and lay the other stack crossways over the top. Fill with apples and syrup.

Fold pastry over to enclose filling. Brush with remaining oil and sprinkle with the remaining extra sugar. Bake for 30–35 minutes or until golden. **SERVES 8**

+ *We recommend using a fresh filo pastry from the fridge section rather than frozen filo pastry, as it is easier to work with.*

Choose any red apple that is in season for the tastiest results.

chapter three
One Dish

A deep, heavy **BAKING DISH** is a *hot contender* for winning your kitchen cupboard's **MVP**. It's just as *at home* cooking slow roasts as it is a glossy upside-down pav. It's also the *perfect vessel* for **MOVEABLE FEASTS** thanks to its deep sides and *sturdy base*, great for travelling from **OVEN TO DINNER PARTY**, or to help transport those cool and crunchy *summer salads*. All that's left to **WASH UP** afterwards is *one dish* – and really, that can soak until the morning ... **CAN'T IT?**

The *much-loved classic* gets a fresh makeover.
HEARTY KALE and *two different cheeses* transform
the humble slice into a MEMORABLE DISH.

the new zucchini slice

850g (about 7) zucchini (courgette), shredded using
    a julienne peeler
½ cup (28g) shredded mint leaves
¼ cup (60ml) extra virgin olive oil
cracked black pepper
3 cups (720g) fresh ricotta
6 eggs
½ cup (125ml) milk
¾ cup (60g) finely grated parmesan
1 tablespoon finely grated lemon rind
3 cups (100g) firmly packed shredded kale leaves
2 green onions (scallions), finely sliced
sea salt and black pepper
prosciutto and rocket (arugula) leaves, to serve

Preheat oven to 200°C (400°F).

Place the zucchini, mint, oil and pepper in a bowl and gently mix[+]. Reserve a quarter of the mixture and set aside.

Place the remaining zucchini mixture, ricotta, eggs, milk, parmesan, lemon rind, kale, green onion, salt and pepper in a bowl and mix to combine.

Place the ricotta mixture into a 20cm x 25cm (8 inch x 10 inch) baking dish and arrange the reserved zucchini mixture around the edge. Bake for 40–45 minutes or until cooked.

Serve warm with prosciutto and rocket leaves.

SERVES 4–6

+ *To ensure your zucchini remains crispy, don't add salt to your zucchini mixture.*

If you don't have a julienne peeler, use a regular vegetable peeler.

TACO NIGHT just got a *whole lot breezier*. Cook your filling and tortillas AT THE SAME TIME and you have already-filled, *crisp and golden* tacos. GENIUS!

all-in-one crispy baked tacos

8 x 20cm (8 inch) flour tortillas
extra virgin olive oil, for brushing
400g cherry tomatoes
½ red onion, finely sliced
2 x 400g cans black beans, rinsed and drained
¼ cup (60g) chipotle chillies in adobo sauce, chillies
    finely chopped and sauce reserved
1½ cups (250g) fresh corn kernels
sea salt and cracked black pepper
1 large avocado, chopped, to serve
1 cup (16g) coriander (cilantro) leaves, to serve
lime cheeks, to serve
lime yoghurt
1 cup (280g) plain thick yoghurt
2 tablespoons lime juice
1 teaspoon finely grated lime rind
1 small clove garlic, crushed
sea salt and cracked black pepper

Preheat oven to 180°C (350°F).

Brush both sides of the tortillas with oil and place them in a deep baking dish. Arrange them together, side-by-side, to form rustic cup-like shapes.

To make the filling, make a small cut in each cherry tomato, squeeze out and discard the seeds. Roughly chop the tomatoes and place them in a bowl with the onion, black beans, chipotles and sauce, corn, salt and pepper.

Spoon into the tortillas and bake for 18–20 minutes or until the tortillas are golden and crisp.

While the tacos are baking, make the lime yoghurt. Mix the yoghurt, lime juice, lime rind, garlic, salt and pepper together in a bowl to combine.

Serve the tacos with avocado, coriander, lime and the lime yoghurt. **SERVES 4**

Feel free to add grated cheese or haloumi to your tacos.

This curry *practically cooks itself*! Just blitz your paste, STIR AND BAKE until the *flavours deepen* into *next-level yum*. Hello, midweek FLAVOUR SAVIOUR.

baked chicken and chickpea coriander curry

6 x 125g chicken thigh fillets, trimmed and halved

2 x 400g cans chickpeas (garbanzo beans), rinsed and drained

1 large eggplant (aubergine), cut into cubes

6 kaffir lime leaves

cooked brown rice, steamed Asian greens, coriander (cilantro) leaves, to serve

coriander curry paste

6 stalks coriander (cilantro), leaves, stems and roots[+]

4 green onions (scallions), roughly chopped

2 long green chillies

2 tablespoons finely grated ginger

2 tablespoons vegetable oil

1 x 400ml can coconut milk

1 tablespoon fish sauce

1 tablespoon lime juice

Preheat oven to 220°C (425°F).

To make the coriander curry paste, place the coriander, green onions, chilli, ginger and oil in a food processor and process until finely chopped. Add the coconut milk, fish sauce and lime juice and blend until smooth.

Place the chicken, chickpeas, eggplant, kaffir lime leaves and coriander curry paste in a deep baking dish and gently mix to coat. Bake for 40–45 minutes or until the chicken is tender and cooked through and the green curry sauce has thickened.

Serve with brown rice, steamed Asian greens and coriander. SERVES 4

+ *Make sure you clean the coriander roots thoroughly.*

Forget stirring at the stovetop — you'll love this new way to make curry!

The STICKY-SWEET marinade and *slow cooking* creates the most MELT-IN-THE-MOUTH lamb, with a *fresh mint sauce* to cut through the richness.

slow-roasted lamb shoulder with mint sauce

1.8kg lamb shoulder on the bone, trimmed
4 green onions (scallions), halved
8 cloves garlic
4 sprigs rosemary
1 cup (250ml) sherry vinegar
1 cup (250ml) good-quality beef stock
1 cup (250ml) cloudy apple juice
sea salt and cracked black pepper
12 baby new potatoes, washed
mint sauce
1 cup (56g) shredded mint leaves
2 tablespoons sherry vinegar
2 tablespoons honey
1 tablespoon wholegrain mustard

Preheat oven to 180°C (350°F).

Place the lamb fat-side down into a large baking dish. Add the green onion, garlic and rosemary.

Combine the sherry vinegar, stock and apple juice and pour over the lamb, then sprinkle with salt and pepper.

Cover the dish with baking paper and aluminium foil and bake for 2½ hours. Remove the cover and carefully turn the lamb over. Add the potatoes to the dish and bake uncovered for a further 1 hour or until the lamb and potatoes are tender.

To make the mint sauce, combine the mint, sherry vinegar, honey and mustard.

Slice the lamb, spoon the mint sauce over the top, and serve with the potatoes and pan juices. SERVES 4

The sherry vinegar can easily be swapped for balsamic.

A *quick kiss of honey and Dijon*, jammy roast pears and fennel, and CRISPY PANCETTA dial this roast up to SUPER-JUICY, *out-of-this-world-tasty* heights.

pancetta-wrapped roast pork with pear and fennel

4 medium fennel bulbs, trimmed and sliced
4 small parsnips, peeled and quartered
3 firm pears, cored and quartered
12 small sage sprigs
2 tablespoons red wine vinegar
2 tablespoons extra virgin olive oil,
   plus extra for drizzling
1 tablespoon honey
sea salt and cracked black pepper
2 x 300g pork fillets
20 slices flat pancetta[+]
honey mustard marinade
¼ cup (70g) Dijon mustard
1 tablespoon honey, extra
sea salt and cracked black pepper

Preheat oven to 220°C (425°F).

Place the fennel, parsnips, pears, sage, vinegar, olive oil, honey, salt and pepper in a large bowl and gently mix to coat. Reserve 4 sage sprigs and set aside.

Place the fruit and vegetables into a large baking dish lined with non-stick baking paper. Roast for 25–30 minutes or until lightly golden.

Meanwhile, make the honey mustard marinade by mixing the mustard, extra honey, salt and pepper in a bowl to combine. Reserve 2 tablespoons of the marinade and set aside.

Brush the pork fillets with the remaining marinade. Wrap each pork fillet in the slices of pancetta, tucking the ends underneath to secure.

Add the pork fillet to the baking dish and brush with the reserved marinade. Top with the reserved sage and drizzle with oil. Roast for 18–22 minutes or until the pork is cooked to your liking.

Slice the pork and serve with the fennel, parsnips, sage and pears, with the pan juices spooned over the top.

SERVES 4

+ *Use flat pancetta instead of the round variety, so that you can wrap it around the pork with ease.*

Wrapping pork in pancetta ups the flavour, locks in moisture and adds a crispy layer of yum!

A HOT GRILL is your hot ticket to *caramelised artichoke edges*, helping release their FULL FLAVOUR potential. Perfect when teamed with *charry chops.*

lamb with artichokes, feta and olives

⅓ cup (80ml) sherry vinegar

2 tablespoons honey

2 tablespoons marjoram or oregano leaves,
    plus 8 sprigs, extra

sea salt and cracked black pepper

8 lamb loin chops

5 large marinated artichoke hearts, halved

2 x 400g cans butter (lima) beans,
    rinsed and drained

200g firm feta, cut into cubes

½ cup (80g) black olives

extra virgin olive oil, for drizzling

green salad or steamed greens, to serve

Preheat oven grill (broiler) to high.

Place the vinegar, honey, marjoram and a generous sprinkle of salt and pepper into a bowl and mix to combine. Add the lamb and toss to coat. Allow to stand for 10 minutes to marinate.

Place the artichokes, beans, feta, olives and extra marjoram into a baking dish. Top with the lamb and marinade and drizzle with oil. Grill for 15–20 minutes or until the lamb is golden and cooked to your liking.

Serve with a simple green salad or steamed greens.

SERVES 4

A one-dish dinner in 30 minutes? Right this way!

Say hello to your new go-to SUMMER SALAD.
A flutter of *fresh ingredients* strikes the PERFECT
BALANCE of cool crunch and *punchy protein.*

lime and soy tofu and cucumber salad

4 Lebanese cucumbers, halved lengthways
   and quartered
1 teaspoon table salt
500g firm silken tofu, sliced
2 avocados, roughly chopped
chilli oil, chopped red onion, toasted sesame seeds
   and coriander (cilantro) leaves, to serve
lime and soy dressing
¼ cup (60ml) lime juice
1½ tablespoons soy sauce
1½ tablespoons black vinegar
1½ tablespoons finely grated ginger
1½ teaspoons sesame oil
1 tablespoon honey

Place the cucumbers in a colander and sprinkle with salt. Set aside for 20 minutes to draw out the moisture.

To make the lime and soy dressing, place the lime juice, soy, vinegar, ginger, sesame oil and honey into a bowl and mix to combine. Add the tofu and allow to stand for 10 minutes to marinate.

Add the cucumber and avocado to the marinated tofu and gently toss to coat.

Divide between bowls and top with chilli oil, red onion, sesame seeds and coriander. **SERVES 4**

All the big flavours of an Asian-inspired stir-fry in a cool, light salad!

Bursting with *bright, zingy,* HERBY GOODNESS, this salad ticks all THE RIGHT BOXES! Serve it with or without the *poached chicken.*

green goddess salad

550g savoy cabbage, sliced into thin wedges
1 cup (16g) mint leaves
½ cup (12g) flat leaf (Italian) parsley leaves
½ cup (10g) small dill sprigs
200g yellow cherry tomatoes, halved
½ cup (80g) roasted almonds, chopped
1 large avocado, cut into large chunks
2 poached chicken breast fillets, sliced (optional)
green goddess dressing
1 large avocado, halved
1 cup (24g) flat-leaf (Italian) parsley leaves
½ cup (24g) chopped chives
¼ cup (60ml) water
2 tablespoons lemon juice
2 tablespoons extra virgin olive oil
sea salt and cracked black pepper

To make the green goddess dressing, place the avocado, parsley, chives, water, lemon juice, oil, salt and pepper into a blender and blend until smooth.

To assemble the salad, place the cabbage, mint, parsley, dill, tomatoes, almonds, avocado, and chicken (if using) on a platter and drizzle with the green goddess dressing.
SERVES 4

You can swap the chicken for tofu or feta.

One Dish

sweet

All the SUMMERTIME SWEETNESS without the fuss!
This recipe *literally turns* the CLASSIC PAV on its head
so there's *no assembly needed.*

upside-down summer pavlova

6 white or yellow peaches or nectarines,
   stones removed and sliced into wedges
6 plums or apricots, stones removed and quartered
⅓ cup (40g) fresh passionfruit pulp
1½ cups (185g) fresh or frozen raspberries
whipped cream, to serve
meringue
225ml egg whites (about 6 eggs)
1 cup (220g) raw caster (superfine) sugar
¼ cup (35g) coconut sugar
1 tablespoon cornflour (cornstarch)
1½ teaspoons white vinegar

Preheat oven to 160°C (325°F).

Place the peaches, plums, passionfruit and raspberries into a deep 25cm x 35cm (10 inch x 13¾ inch) baking dish. Set aside.

To make the meringue, place the egg whites in the bowl of an electric mixer and whisk on high speed until soft peaks form.

Combine the caster sugar and coconut sugar in a bowl. Add the mixed sugars to the egg whites, 1 tablespoon at a time, whisking until each addition has dissolved before adding more.

Once all the sugar has been added, scrape down the sides of the bowl and whisk for a further 10–15 minutes or until thick and glossy.

Place the cornflour and vinegar in a small bowl and mix until smooth. Add the cornflour mixture to the egg white mixture and gently fold through.

Spoon the meringue mixture over the top of the fruits. Reduce oven temperature to 140°C (275°F) and bake for 1 hour or until the meringue has crisp edges. Serve warm or chilled with whipped cream. **SERVES 6-8**

I recommend a freestyle approach to the fruits you use in this pavlova — just look to the season for inspiration!

This is a **DELICIOUS WAY** to show off *sweet seasonal fruits!* Elderflower gives this *crunchy-topped* cobbler a burst of SPRING SUNSHINE.

elderflower berry cobbler

8 cups (1kg) frozen mixed berries
2 tablespoons cornflour (cornstarch)
1 tablespoon chia seeds
¼ cup (60ml) elderflower cordial
1–2 tablespoons raw caster (superfine) sugar, for sprinkling
coconut topping
¾ cup (110g) plain (all-purpose) wholemeal (whole-wheat) flour
¾ cup (110g) plain (all-purpose) flour
1 cup (80g) desiccated coconut
¾ cup (110g) coconut sugar
3 teaspoons baking powder
100g cold unsalted butter, chopped
¾ cup (180ml) buttermilk
3 teaspoons vanilla extract

Preheat oven to 180°C (350°F).

Place the mixed berries, cornflour, chia and elderflower cordial into a deep 12-cup-capacity (3 litre) round baking dish and mix to combine.

To make the coconut topping, place the flours, coconut, coconut sugar and baking powder in a bowl and mix to combine. Add the butter and rub the mixture together using your fingertips to combine. Add the buttermilk and vanilla and mix to combine.

Add spoonfuls of the coconut topping over the elderflower berries and sprinkle with caster sugar. Bake for 1 hour or until puffed and golden. Serve warm. **SERVES 6**

You can use just about any seasonal fruit that you have on hand in this cobbler.

Coconut gives this **EXPRESS CRUMBLE** its toasty, chewy, **SUPER-TASTY** edge. It's the *perfect golden* topping for all those warm **STICKY FRUITS**.

any fruit coconut crumble

1kg pears, cored and sliced
300g strawberries, trimmed and halved
⅓ cup (60g) crystallised ginger, chopped
¼ cup (55g) raw caster (superfine) sugar
crumble topping
2 cups (160g) desiccated coconut
2 cups (150g) shredded coconut
¾ cup (165g) raw caster (superfine) sugar
4 large egg whites, lightly whisked

Preheat oven to 160°C (325°F).

Combine the fruit, crystallised ginger and sugar together and place in a deep 18cm x 26cm (7 inch x 10¼ inch) baking dish. Bake for 30 minutes.

While the fruit is cooking, make the crumble topping. Place the desiccated coconut, shredded coconut, sugar and egg whites in a bowl and mix to combine.

Spoon the topping over the fruit and bake for a further 30–35 minutes or until golden. **SERVES 6-8**

+ *You can choose your own fruit combinations.*
- *For apple, rhubarb and raspberry, simply use 3 sliced apples, 420g chopped rhubarb, and 2 cups (250g) frozen raspberries.*
- *For apple and raspberry, simply use 6 sliced red apples and 3 cups (375g) frozen raspberries.*
- *For pear and blueberry, simply use 4 sliced green pears and 2 cups (250g) frozen blueberries.*
- *For apple, strawberry and ginger, simply use 3 sliced apples, 3 cups (375g) fresh or frozen strawberries, halved, and 2 tablespoons finely grated ginger.*

True to its name, this is my version of a choose-your-own-adventure crumble.

My super-fast, super-zesty BLEND-AND-BAKE pudding makes the *fluffiest base* for glossy, MARSHMALLOW-Y MERINGUE. *Pass the spoon!*

lemon meringue pudding

1½ cups (375ml) milk
1½ cups (375ml) coconut milk
¾ cup (60g) desiccated coconut
50g unsalted butter, melted
2 eggs
4 egg yolks
½ cup (75g) plain (all-purpose) flour
1 cup (220g) caster (superfine) sugar
½ cup (125ml) lemon juice
2 teaspoons finely grated lemon rind
meringue
150ml egg whites (about 4 egg whites)
¾ cup (165g) caster (superfine) sugar

Preheat oven to 160°C (325°F).

Place the milk, coconut milk, coconut, butter, eggs, yolks, flour, sugar, lemon juice and rind into a blender and blend until smooth.

Pour the mixture into a 6-cup (1.5 litre) capacity shallow baking dish. Bake for 30–35 minutes or until just set. Remove from the oven.

Increase oven temperature to 220°C (425°F).

To make the meringue, place the egg whites into the bowl of an electric mixer and whisk on high speed until soft peaks form.

Add the sugar, 1 tablespoon at a time, whisking until each addition has dissolved before adding more.

Once all the sugar has been added, scrape down the sides of the bowl and whisk for a further 10 minutes or until thick and glossy.

Spoon the meringue onto the pudding base and bake for a further 5 minutes or until the meringue is lightly golden. **SERVES 6**

Use fresh room temperature eggs for the fluffiest meringue peaks.

With its crisp cake-like crust and SUPER-SOFT centre, this cake truly is the *sweetest of both worlds.* Serve it for dessert or AFTERNOON TEA.

rhubarb almond pudding cake

4 eggs
1 teaspoon vanilla extract
1 teaspoon rosewater
1½ cups (360ml) buttermilk
1 tablespoon finely grated orange rind
2½ cups (300g) almond meal (ground almonds)
2 tablespoons cornflour (cornstarch)
¾ cup (165g) raw caster (superfine) sugar,
   plus extra
5 stalks rhubarb, trimmed and halved lengthways
1 tablespoon light agave syrup or pure maple syrup

Preheat oven to 180°C (350°F).

Place the eggs, vanilla, rosewater, buttermilk and orange rind into a jug and whisk to combine.

Place the almond meal, cornflour and sugar into a bowl and mix to combine.

Pour the buttermilk mixture into the almond mixture and mix to combine.

Pour mixture into a deep 25cm (10 inch) 6-cup (1.5 litre) capacity round baking dish.

Top the almond mixture with the rhubarb and brush well with agave syrup. Sprinkle with extra sugar.

Bake for 40 minutes or until the pudding cake is just firm and the rhubarb is soft. **SERVES 4-6**

Swap rhubarb for berries or even peaches or nectarines if in season.

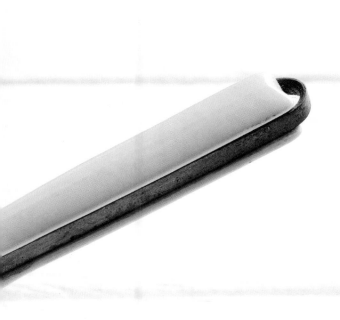

chapter four
One Pot

There's so MUCH MAGIC that happens inside your *humble pot* or saucepan. We're not just talking about SIMMERING STEWS and bubbling braises but *better-for-you bread*, soups that are cosier than your FAVOURITE SWEATER, and fall-apart brisket. *Deep pots* are great for giving pasta the *elbow room* it needs, while HEAVY-BASED POTS will gift you with those *crisp and even* GOLDEN CRUSTS and *travel seamlessly* to the oven when you need them to. ONE POT *with the lot* is all you need!

Ready in under 20, this *zesty tangle* of all the GOOD THINGS has become our *go-to studio lunch.* Finish with a light shower of cheese or a MILKY BURRATA orb.

simple super greens pasta

400g dried wholemeal (whole-wheat) pasta
¼ cup (60ml) extra virgin olive oil
4 cloves garlic, sliced
1 long red chilli, sliced
5 cups (175g) firmly packed shredded kale leaves
2 zucchini (courgette), grated
2½ cups (60g) baby spinach leaves
½ cup (60g) sauerkraut
⅓ cup (18g) shredded mint leaves
1 tablespoon finely grated lemon rind
sea salt and cracked black pepper
buffalo mozzarella, burrata or finely grated parmesan
   and lemon wedges, to serve

Cook the pasta in a large saucepan of boiling salted water for 8 minutes or until al dente. Drain, reserving 1 cup (250ml) pasta water, and set aside.

Return the saucepan to medium heat and add the oil, garlic and chilli. Cook for 2–3 minutes or until the garlic is soft. Add the kale and zucchini and cook, stirring for 3 minutes or until the kale has wilted.

Add the spinach, sauerkraut, mint, lemon rind, salt and pepper and stir through. Add the pasta and toss to combine, adding a generous splash of the reserved pasta water if needed.

Serve the pasta with buffalo mozzarella, burrata or parmesan, and a squeeze of lemon. SERVES 4

Sauerkraut is a master stroke of flavour in these pasta bowls.

SCAN THIS CODE FOR RECIPE VIDEO

My sticky SET-AND-FORGET roast chicken will become your new *family favourite.* All the JUICY FLAVOUR without the fuss – *yes please!*

balsamic pot roast chicken

½ cup (125ml) balsamic vinegar
1 cup (250ml) good-quality chicken stock
¼ cup (60g) firmly packed brown sugar
8 sprigs oregano
6 cloves garlic, halved
1 x 1.6kg whole chicken
sea salt and cracked black pepper
1kg medium roasting potatoes, cut into large chunks
600g parsnips (about 3), peeled and halved
extra virgin olive oil, for drizzling

Preheat oven to 220°C (425°F).

Place the balsamic, stock, sugar, oregano and garlic into a deep ovenproof saucepan. Sprinkle the chicken with salt and pepper and add to the pan, breast-side down. Add the potatoes and parsnips and drizzle with oil. Cover with a tight-fitting lid, place in the oven and bake for 45–50 minutes.

Remove the lid and carefully turn the chicken over. Baste the chicken with the pan juices and cook for a further 10–15 minutes or until golden and cooked through.
SERVES 4

You can swap the parsnips for carrots – either way, this easy pot roast is a meal in itself!

SCAN THIS CODE FOR RECIPE VIDEO

SUPER-FRESH and bursting with *bright lemony flavour,* with HEARTY QUINOA dumplings bobbing around, my *new chicken soup* is like a warm, COMFORTING HUG.

lemon chicken dumpling soup

2 tablespoons extra virgin olive oil

2 onions, chopped

4 cloves garlic, sliced

1 tablespoon tarragon leaves

8 cups (2 litres) good-quality chicken stock

12 stalks (240g) cavolo nero (Tuscan kale),
  stems removed

2 tablespoons lemon juice

sea salt and cracked black pepper

2 cups (280g) cooked quinoa

finely grated parmesan, to serve

lemon chicken dumplings

500g chicken mince

¾ cup (100g) cooked quinoa

⅓ cup (25g) finely grated parmesan

2 teaspoons finely grated lemon rind

¼ teaspoon chilli flakes

1 egg

1 tablespoon chopped tarragon

sea salt and cracked black pepper

To make the lemon chicken dumplings, mix the chicken mince, quinoa, parmesan, lemon rind, chilli flakes, egg, tarragon, salt and pepper in a bowl to combine.

Using wet hands, roll heaped tablespoons of the mixture into 20 balls. Place on a tray, cover and refrigerate until needed.

To make the soup, place the oil in a large saucepan over medium heat. Add the onions and cook for 5 minutes or until soft. Add the garlic and tarragon and cook for 2 minutes or until fragrant. Add the stock and bring to the boil.

Cover with a lid, reduce heat and simmer for 5 minutes. Remove lid, add the lemon chicken dumplings and gently simmer for 6–7 minutes. Add the cavolo nero and cook for 2 minutes or until the balls are cooked through and the cavolo nero is soft. Stir the lemon juice through and sprinkle with salt and pepper.

To serve, divide the cooked quinoa between bowls and top with the cavolo nero, lemon chicken dumplings and soup. Sprinkle with grated parmesan and cracked black pepper. SERVES 4

Nice-for-you quinoa and chicken dumplings make this soup satisfying on so many levels!

A big, colourful, SPICE-KISSED bowl of soup that is equal parts *delicious and restorative* is exactly what you need when the WEATHER COOLS DOWN.

spiced turmeric, sweet potato and carrot soup

2 tablespoons extra virgin olive oil
2 onions, chopped
2 teaspoons ground turmeric
1 teaspoon ground cumin
2 tablespoons finely grated ginger
750g sweet potato (kumara), peeled and cut
    into 2cm (¾ inch) pieces
4 carrots, peeled, quartered lengthways and cut
    into 2cm (¾ inch) pieces
2 x 400ml cans coconut milk
2 cups (500ml) good-quality chicken stock
1 cup (16g) coriander (cilantro) leaves, chopped
sea salt and cracked black pepper
sliced red chilli, to serve

Place a large saucepan over medium-high heat.
    Add the oil, onion, turmeric, cumin and ginger and cook for 3 minutes, stirring constantly, until soft.
    Add the sweet potato, carrot, coconut milk and stock and simmer for 30–35 minutes or until the vegetables are tender.
    Add the coriander, salt and pepper and stir through. Divide soup between bowls and top with sliced chilli.
SERVES 4

The turmeric and ginger base gives this soup nourishing powers!

Crack through **CRISP AND FLAKY** pastry to reveal
creamy, zesty chicken and **NOURISHING GREENS.**
Comfort food made so *easy and delicious.*

creamy lemon chicken pot pie

store-bought puff pastry
2 tablespoons extra virgin olive oil
2 leeks, thinly sliced
1 tablespoon lemon thyme leaves
½ cup (80g) brown rice flour
5 chicken thigh fillets (about 600g), trimmed
    and chopped
1 tablespoon finely grated lemon rind
1¼ cups (310ml) good-quality chicken stock
3½ cups (140g) firmly packed finely shredded
    cavolo nero (Tuscan kale) leaves
½ cup (125g) crème fraîche
sea salt and cracked black pepper
1 egg, lightly whisked

Preheat oven to 200°C (400°F).

Cut the pastry into a circle to fit the top of an 18cm (7 inch) deep 8-cup-capacity (2 litre) ovenproof saucepan. Set pastry aside in the fridge to keep chilled.

Heat the saucepan over medium heat. Add the oil, leeks and lemon thyme and cook for 4 minutes or until the leek is soft and golden.

Place the flour and chicken in a bowl and toss to coat. Shake off the excess flour. Add the chicken to the pan and cook for 4–5 minutes.

Add the lemon rind and stock and bring to the boil. Reduce heat to low and simmer for 10 minutes or until the chicken is tender.

Add the cavolo nero and cook, stirring for 5–7 minutes or until the greens are wilted and the sauce has thickened. Remove from the heat, add the crème fraîche, salt and pepper and stir to combine.

Place the pastry over the pan to enclose it and brush with the egg. Bake for 25–30 minutes or until the pastry is golden. **SERVES 4**

Swap crème fraîche for sour cream, if you prefer.

You'll JUST LOVE this light and textural pasta, laced with *crunchy pistachios* and GOOD-FOR-YOU edamame, then lifted with *super-fresh* mint.

smashed edamame and mint pasta

400g dried orecchiette pasta
2 cloves garlic
3 cups (420g) frozen shelled edamame beans, thawed
2 tablespoons finely grated lemon rind
2 tablespoons lemon juice
¼ cup (60ml) extra virgin olive oil
2 cups (112g) shredded mint leaves
sea salt and cracked black pepper
¼ cup (35g) pistachios, roughly chopped
finely grated parmesan and baby mint leaves, to serve

Cook the pasta and garlic in a large saucepan of boiling salted water for 10 minutes or until al dente. Drain the pasta, remove the garlic and mash with a fork. Set aside.

Place the edamame in the saucepan and cover with hot water. Blanch for 2 minutes or until the beans are soft. Drain edamame and return to the pan. Using a potato masher or fork, roughly mash the edamame in the pan.

Return the pasta to the saucepan with the reserved crushed garlic, lemon rind, lemon juice, oil, mint, salt and pepper and toss to combine.

Spoon into bowls, sprinkle with pistachios and serve with parmesan and extra mint. **SERVES 4**

You could easily make this with long wholemeal spaghetti if you wanted to.

CELERIAC SHINES in this *silky soup* bursting with warm, EARTHY TONES and a sprinkle of toasted hazelnuts for *that crunch factor.*

celeriac and fennel soup with hazelnuts and tarragon

¼ cup (60ml) extra virgin olive oil

⅓ cup (45g) hazelnuts, chopped, to serve

8 sprigs tarragon, to serve

650g (about 2) fennel bulbs, sliced

2 brown onions, sliced

6 cloves garlic, finely chopped

1.2kg (about 2 large) celeriac (celery root), peeled and chopped

5½ cups (1.4 litres) good-quality chicken or vegetable stock

sea salt and cracked black pepper

buttermilk, to serve

Place a large saucepan over medium heat.

Add 2 tablespoons oil and the hazelnuts and cook for 2 minutes or until toasted. Remove from the pan and set aside. Add the tarragon and cook for 15–30 seconds. Remove from the pan and set aside.

Add the remaining oil, fennel and onion to the pan and cook for 15 minutes or until slightly golden.

Add the garlic and cook for 1 minute, then add the celeriac and cook for 5 minutes.

Add the stock and bring to the boil. Reduce heat to low and simmer, covered, for 30 minutes or until the vegetables are tender. Remove from the heat.

Using a handheld blender, blend the mixture until smooth. Sprinkle with salt and pepper.

Divide soup between bowls and top with toasted hazelnuts, tarragon and buttermilk. **SERVES 4**

Serve this soup with any accompaniments you like — sage, thyme, homemade sourdough croutons — you decide.

I love this playful, *punchy pasta,* inspired by our *favourite spicy cocktail.* It's the PERFECT BALANCE of heat, sweet and YUM!

pasta with bloody mary sauce

400g dried wholemeal (whole-wheat) spaghetti
⅓ cup (80ml) extra virgin olive oil
500g cherry tomatoes
2 long red chillies, chopped
8 cloves garlic, sliced
½ cup (125ml) vodka or gin
1 tablespoon Worcestershire sauce
½ teaspoon Tabasco sauce, to taste
sea salt and cracked black pepper
celery leaves and finely grated parmesan, to serve

Cook the spaghetti in a large saucepan of boiling salted water for 8 minutes or until al dente. Drain, reserving ½ cup (125ml) of pasta water and set aside.

Return saucepan to high heat. Add 2 tablespoons oil and tomatoes and cook for 3 minutes, stirring occasionally, until the tomato skins are slightly charred.

Reduce heat to medium. Add the chilli and garlic and cook for 1–2 minutes.

Add the vodka, reserved pasta water, Worcestershire, Tabasco, remaining oil, salt and pepper and mix to combine. Return the pasta to the pan and toss for 1 minute or until warmed through. Serve the pasta with celery leaves and parmesan. **SERVES 4**

Just like your favourite savoury cocktail, adjust your Tabasco to suit your taste.

Tender, FALL-APART brisket is *upflavoured* with Sriracha and honey, then brightened with a ZINGY PICKLE in these *super juicy* burgers.

honey sriracha brisket burgers

750g beef brisket, trimmed
sea salt and cracked black pepper
1 tablespoon extra virgin olive oil
2 onions, sliced
4 sprigs oregano
2 tablespoons sriracha hot chilli sauce
2 tablespoons honey
1 cup (250ml) tomato passata (puree)
1 cup (250ml) good-quality beef stock
mixed seeded burger buns, halved
mayonnaise, coriander (cilantro) leaves and fries,
    to serve
quick pickled carrot
4 carrots, thinly sliced into ribbons using a peeler
2 tablespoons apple cider vinegar
2 teaspoons honey

Place a large saucepan over medium-high heat.

Sprinkle the brisket with salt and pepper and cook in the saucepan for 2–3 minutes each side or until evenly browned all over. Remove from the pan and set aside.

Reduce heat to medium. Add the oil, onions and oregano and cook for 5 minutes or until soft. Add the sriracha, honey, passata and stock and bring to a simmer.

Add the brisket, cover with a tight-fitting lid and cook over medium-low heat for 3 hours, turning it halfway, until the brisket is tender and falls apart. Shred using forks and toss the brisket through the sauce.

Just before serving, make the quick pickled carrots. Place the carrots, vinegar and honey in a bowl and toss to combine.

Spread each bun base with mayonnaise and top with the quick pickled carrot, coriander and brisket, then sandwich with the bun top. Serve with fries, if you like.
SERVES 4–6

Pile this honey sriracha brisket into tortillas instead of burger buns, if you like.

Six ingredients is all you need for this simple ONE-POT PASTA. Silky strands are coated in a *buttery miso sauce* that EXPLODES WITH FLAVOUR.

silky miso pasta

400g dried spaghetti
¼ cup (55g) white (shiro) miso paste
50g unsalted butter, cut into cubes
1 cup (80g) finely grated parmesan, plus extra
   to serve
5½ cups (140g) baby spinach leaves
furikake, to serve[+]

Cook the spaghetti in a large saucepan of boiling salted water for 8 minutes or until al dente.

Drain the pasta, reserving 1½ cups (375ml) of the pasta water. Add the miso to the pasta water in the pan and whisk until the miso has dissolved.

Return pasta to the pan and cook over medium heat for 3–4 minutes or until the pasta is coated in the sauce.

Remove from the heat, add the butter and mix to coat. Stir the parmesan and baby spinach through.

Serve the pasta topped with furikake and finely grated parmesan. **SERVES 4**

+ *Furikake is a Japanese seasoning typically made from sesame seeds, nori, salt and sugar. Replace it with shredded nori sheets and sesame seeds, if you like.*

Miso is the flavour saviour your weeknight pasta bowl is missing!

Farro is the GOOD-FOR-YOU grain that gives this risotto its *nutty, chewy magic*. Then, CRISPY SAGE and almonds take it to *next-level yum.*

farro, cauliflower and sage risotto

¼ cup (60ml) extra virgin olive oil
½ cup (8g) sage leaves, to serve
½ cup (80g) roughly chopped almonds, to serve
1 onion, finely chopped
2 cloves garlic, sliced
½ cup (125ml) dry white wine
500g cauliflower florets, trimmed and finely chopped
1½ cups (320g) farro
½ cup (100g) arborio rice
6 cups (1.5 litres) hot good-quality chicken
    or vegetable stock
1½ cups (375ml) milk
½ cup (40g) finely grated parmesan
sea salt and cracked black pepper
300g washed rind cheese or brie, thickly sliced,
    to serve

Place a large deep saucepan over medium heat. Add half the oil, sage and almonds and cook for 3–4 minutes or until crisp. Remove from the pan and set aside.

Add the remaining oil, onion, and garlic and cook, stirring occasionally, for 4–5 minutes or until softened. Add the wine and cook for 1 minute.

Add the cauliflower, farro and rice and cook, stirring for 1–2 minutes. Reduce heat to medium-low and cook, stirring frequently.

Add the stock, 1 cup (250ml) at a time, allowing each cup to absorb before adding more, stirring frequently for 50–55 minutes. Once absorbed, add the milk and cook, stirring until the rice is creamy. Add the parmesan, salt and pepper and stir to combine.

Divide the risotto between bowls and top with the washed rind cheese, crispy sage and almonds. **SERVES 4–6**

If you don't have farro, you could use freekeh. You could also replace washed rind cheese with extra parmesan.

I love using smart, BETTER-FOR-YOU ingredients where I can. Buttermilk *brings the creaminess* to this fresh, CRUNCHY PASTA, while keeping it *nice and light.*

creamy lemon and brussels pasta

400g dried wholemeal (whole-wheat) pasta
2 tablespoons extra virgin olive oil
1 leek, finely sliced
600g brussels sprouts (about 18), shredded,
    plus extra leaves to serve
2 tablespoons finely grated lemon rind
2½ cups (600ml) buttermilk
1 tablespoon lemon juice
sea salt and cracked black pepper
⅓ cup (45g) pistachios, roasted and chopped,
    to serve
200g goat's cheese or finely grated parmesan,
    to serve
lemon cheeks, to serve

Cook the pasta in a large saucepan of boiling salted water for 8 minutes or until al dente. Drain and set aside.

Return saucepan to medium-high heat, add the oil and leek and cook for 5 minutes or until golden.

Add the brussels sprouts and lemon rind and cook for 2–3 minutes. Add the pasta, buttermilk and lemon juice to the pan and cook, stirring for 2–3 minutes or until heated through. Sprinkle with salt and pepper.

Serve the pasta with extra brussels sprouts leaves, pistachios, goat's cheese or parmesan, and lemon cheeks.
SERVES 4

Wholemeal pasta gives this bowl a delicious earthy flavour, but you could also use regular pasta if you prefer.

This has become my favourite STANDBY SOUP. It's so fresh, zingy and *loaded with green goodness*, with a swirl of my PUNCHY TAHINI sauce for a *flavour kick.*

spinach soup with lemon and tahini

1 tablespoon extra virgin olive oil
2 onions, chopped
6 cups (1.5 litres) good-quality vegetable
   or chicken stock
400g baby spinach leaves
1 cup (16g) coriander (cilantro) leaves
1 cup (24g) flat-leaf (Italian) parsley leaves
1 cup (16g) mint leaves
2 tablespoons hulled tahini
1 tablespoon finely grated lemon rind
sea salt and cracked black pepper
sumac, to serve
tahini sauce
⅓ cup (90g) hulled tahini
¼ cup (60ml) lemon juice
½ teaspoon ground cumin
2 tablespoons water

Place a large saucepan over medium heat. Add the oil and onion and cook for 5 minutes or until soft. Add the stock and bring to the boil, then simmer for 5 minutes.

Add the spinach, coriander, parsley and mint and cook for 2 minutes or until the leaves are wilted. Add the tahini, lemon rind, salt and pepper and stir to combine.

Using a handheld blender, blend until smooth.

To make the tahini sauce, place the tahini, lemon juice, cumin and water in a bowl and stir to combine.

Divide soup between bowls, swirl the tahini sauce through and sprinkle with sumac. **SERVES 4**

Make a batch of this soup on the weekend and it will keep giving throughout the week.

Glossy rainbow chard is the FRESHER-THAN-FRESH stand-in for pastry in this *stunning pie*. Every mouthful POPS WITH FLAVOUR, texture and wow!

lamb and quinoa rainbow chard pie

extra virgin olive oil, for brushing
10–12 large stalks rainbow chard or silverbeet
   (Swiss chard), trimmed and lightly blanched
lemon wedges, to serve
pie filling
1 tablespoon extra virgin olive oil
1 onion, chopped
500g lamb mince
sea salt and cracked black pepper
3 eggs, lightly whisked
2 tablespoons hulled tahini
2 teaspoons finely grated orange rind
¼ cup (60ml) orange juice
3 cups (420g) cooked quinoa
¾ cup (40g) chopped flat-leaf (Italian) parsley leaves
¼ cup (12g) chopped dill leaves
⅓ cup (45g) slivered almonds, toasted
⅓ cup (45g) currants
½ teaspoon chilli flakes
250g feta, broken into large chunks

Place a large shallow ovenproof saucepan over medium-high heat.

To make the pie filling, add the oil and onion and cook for 3 minutes or until soft. Add the lamb mince, salt and pepper and cook for 5 minutes or until well browned.

Place the eggs, tahini, orange rind and juice into a bowl and mix to combine. Add the lamb mixture, quinoa, parsley, dill, almonds, currants and chilli and mix to combine. Add the feta and gently mix to combine.

Preheat oven to 200°C (400°F).

Wipe the pan clean and brush with a little oil. Lay the chard leaves around the pan so they overlap, allowing the leaves to overhang the dish. Trim the stems if needed.

Spoon the lamb quinoa mixture onto the chard and fold the excess leaves over to enclose the filling. Use the remaining chard to cover the top of the filling. Brush with oil and cover with baking paper and aluminium foil.

Bake the pie for 30 minutes or until heated through. Slice the pie and serve with lemon wedges. **SERVE 4-6**

Choose large rainbow chard leaves to help you easily assemble this showstopper pie.

Inspired by the CLASSIC HAINANESE CHICKEN, this WEEKNIGHT-FRIENDLY *one-pot version* has all the comforting, *fragrant flavour* we love from the original.

lucky pot ginger chicken

2 tablespoons vegetable oil
6 cloves garlic, finely chopped
1 long green chilli, sliced
12 thin slices ginger (about 25g)
4 green onions (scallions), thickly sliced
2 cups (360g) brown basmati rice, rinsed
3 cups (750ml) good-quality chicken stock
1 cup (250ml) water
2 tablespoons soy sauce
8 x 125g small chicken thigh fillets, trimmed
250g snow peas (mange tout), shredded
soy sauce, thinly sliced green chilli, coriander (cilantro)
  leaves and finely grated ginger, to serve

Place a large saucepan over medium heat. Add the oil, garlic, chilli, ginger, green onion and rice and cook, stirring for 4 minutes, or until the rice is slightly toasted.

Add the stock, water and soy sauce and stir to combine. Add the chicken on top of the rice and bring to a simmer. Cover with a tight-fitting lid and reduce the heat to medium-low. Cook for 20 minutes, then remove from the heat.

Working quickly so that heat doesn't escape, carefully lift the lid of the pan and scatter the snow peas over the chicken and rice. Replace lid and allow to stand for 10 minutes.

Serve with soy sauce, green chilli, coriander leaves and grated ginger. **SERVES 4**

You can easily leave out the chilli for a wholesome family-friendly meal.

chapter four

One Pot

sweet

A sticky, SPRITZY DESSERT that is drenched in
all the best parts of your *favourite aperitivo* cocktail,
for when you need a taste of LA DOLCE VITA.

aperol spritz peaches

4 peaches
3 cups (750ml) prosecco
1 cup (250ml) Aperol[+]
½ cup (110g) raw caster (superfine) sugar
2 vanilla bean pods, ends trimmed
6 thick strips orange peel
vanilla bean yoghurt or ice-cream, to serve

Place the peaches into a medium saucepan and cover
with boiling water. Allow to stand for 5 minutes, drain and
gently slip the skins off.

Return the saucepan with the peaches to medium-high
heat. Add the prosecco, Aperol, sugar, vanilla and orange
peel and bring to the boil. Reduce heat to low and simmer
for 5 minutes. Remove peaches and reduce the syrup for
8–10 minutes or until it has thickened slightly.

Top peaches with vanilla bean yoghurt or ice-cream and
a drizzle of syrup. SERVES 4
+ Aperol is a bitter orange liquor. You can swap it for
Campari, if you prefer.

You can adjust the amount of Aperol to suit your taste.

This could be *the quickest dessert* you'll ever make! Boozy, spiced and SERIOUSLY SYRUPY apples, ready in *under 10 minutes*. Yes please!

appletini compote

½ cup (125ml) water
¼ cup (60ml) gin
¼ cup (60ml) pure maple syrup
1 cinnamon stick
thick peel of 1 lemon
¼ cup (60ml) lemon juice
2 red apples, sliced horizontally into 8mm
   (⅜ inch) rounds
lemon sorbet, to serve

Place the water, gin, maple syrup, cinnamon, lemon peel and juice in a medium saucepan over medium heat and stir to combine. Add the apples and bring to a simmer. Cook the apples for 5 minutes, turning occasionally so that they cook evenly.

Serve warm or chilled with lemon sorbet. **SERVES 4**

You could serve this appletini with vanilla ice–cream if you preferred.

It tastes so *creamy and comforting*, but it's actually full of SUPER NICE stuff. You'll love the gentle *citrusy flavour* and CHIA GOODNESS in these dessert bowls.

vanilla and almond rice pudding

¾ cup (150g) arborio rice

4 cups (1 litre) milk or nut milk, plus extra
  to serve

½ cup (110g) raw caster (superfine) sugar

2 thick slices orange peel

1 vanilla bean, split and seeds scraped

2 tablespoons white chia seeds

coconut sugar, to serve

Place the rice, milk, sugar, orange peel, vanilla bean and seeds in a large saucepan over high heat and bring to the boil. Reduce heat to low, cover and cook, stirring occasionally, for 20 minutes or until the rice is tender. Add chia and stir for 3–5 minutes or until thickened.

Allow to stand for 5 minutes, then remove the vanilla bean. Serve with coconut sugar and milk. **SERVES 4**

If you prefer a spiced-up rice pudding, add a sprinkle of ground cinnamon on top.

SILKY AND RICH, with a nutty, *glass-shattering* crumb, these LITTLE POPS OF YUM make the dreamiest chocolate treat or deliciously *edible gift.*

chocolate coconut truffles with pistachio praline

250g dark (70% cocoa) chocolate, chopped
1 cup (250ml) thick coconut cream
pistachio praline
½ cup (110g) raw caster (superfine) sugar
¼ cup (35g) pistachios, finely chopped

Place the chocolate and coconut cream in a saucepan over low heat and stir for 2–3 minutes or until smooth. Spoon into a bowl and chill in the fridge for 1 hour or until firm enough to roll into balls.

To make the pistachio praline, heat a medium saucepan over medium heat. Add the sugar and cook without stirring for 5–7 minutes or until the sugar has melted and is dark golden brown.

Place the pistachios on a tray lined with non-stick baking paper. Carefully pour the melted sugar over the pistachios and allow to cool completely.

Once the praline has set, break it into pieces and place in a mortar. Pound with a pestle until fine[+].

To assemble, roll tablespoons of the chilled chocolate coconut mixture into balls and then roll in the praline crumb. Refrigerate for 10 minutes or until firm. Keep in an airtight container in the fridge. **MAKES 24**

+ *If you don't have a mortar and pestle, you could place the praline pieces between sheets of baking paper and crush with a rolling pin.*

A good-quality chocolate will give you the tastiest truffles.

Laced with soft, SWEET FIGS and crunchy walnuts, this is the tastiest, *nice-for-you*, NO-FUSS BREAD that even *first-time bakers* can master!

fig, walnut and honey loaf

2½ cups (625ml) warm water
1 tablespoon honey
1 teaspoon dry yeast
3½ cups (560g) plain (all-purpose) white spelt flour
3½ cups (420g) plain (all-purpose) wholemeal
   (whole-wheat) spelt flour, plus extra for dusting
2 teaspoons ground cinnamon
2 teaspoons sea salt flakes
½ cup (125ml) extra virgin olive oil
¼ cup (90g) honey, extra
2 cups (320g) chopped soft dried figs
2 cups (200g) roughly chopped walnuts
fresh ricotta and honey, to serve

Place the water, honey and yeast in a medium jug and mix to combine. Set aside until bubbles form on the surface.

Place the flours, cinnamon and salt in the bowl of an electric mixer with the dough hook attached.

Knead on low speed, gradually adding the yeast mixture, oil and extra honey. Knead for 10 minutes or until the dough is smooth. Add the figs and walnuts and gently knead through.

Transfer the dough to a large lightly greased bowl and cover with plastic wrap. Set aside in a warm place for 1½–2 hours or until the dough has doubled in size.

Preheat oven to 250°C (480°F). Heat a deep 24cm (9½ inch) ovenproof heavy-based saucepan and tight-fitting lid in the oven for 30 minutes.

Lightly dust the hot pan with flour. Lightly dust a clean work surface with flour and turn the dough out. Shape into a round and, using floured hands, carefully place the dough into the saucepan. Dust with flour and score the top of the dough with a small sharp knife. Cover with the lid and bake in the oven for 30 minutes.

Reduce oven temperature to 220°C (425°F). Remove the lid and bake the loaf for a further 10 minutes or until golden and the bread sounds hollow when tapped.

Serve with ricotta and honey. MAKES 1

Swap figs for chopped soft fresh dates if you have those at home.

Flavour Starters

I like to think of these as 'JUST-ADD-FRESH' meal prep. Build these flavour starters ahead of time and they'll add *punch and pop* to your next meal IN A FLASH. There's nothing better than opening your fridge to find a jar of *super-tasty,* READY-TO-GO marinade or curry paste, on hand to *upflavour* your next soup, stir-fry or salmon dish in just minutes. I call it the ultimate 'PAY-IT-FORWARD' in the kitchen! *Future you* will love you for it.

This **LIP-SMACKING,** nose-tingling paste finds the *sweet spot* between punchy, **SPICY AND CREAMY.** Your midweek *flavour saviour* has arrived!

red chilli coconut paste

½ cup (125ml) vegetable oil

8 long red chillies, chopped

12 cloves garlic, chopped

6 stalks lemongrass, white parts only, chopped

15 kaffir lime leaves, chopped

110g ginger, peeled and chopped

6 stalks coriander (cilantro), leaves, stems and roots+, chopped

1½ cups (375ml) coconut cream

⅓ cup (80ml) fish sauce

½ cup (110g) raw caster (superfine) sugar

Place the oil, chilli, garlic, lemongrass, kaffir lime leaves, ginger and coriander in a food processor and process until finely chopped.

Heat a medium saucepan over medium-high heat. Add the coconut cream and cook for 8 minutes, stirring occasionally, until the coconut cream has reduced and appears separated. Add the chilli mixture and cook for 3 minutes.

Reduce heat to medium and add fish sauce and sugar. Cook for 12–15 minutes or until the paste is caramelised and the red oil starts to separate.

You can keep this paste in an airtight container in the fridge for up to 8 weeks. **MAKES 3 CUPS (840G)**

+ *Be sure to clean the coriander roots thoroughly.*

If you prefer a mild and mellow paste, simply remove the seeds from the chillies.

coconut pumpkin, prawn and rice noodle soup

chilli coconut chicken stir-fry

coconut pumpkin, prawn and rice noodle soup

½ cup (140g) red chilli coconut paste (see *recipe* p198)
2 cups (500ml) coconut cream
3½ cups (875ml) good-quality chicken stock
1.2kg butternut pumpkin, peeled and chopped
    into cubes
12 green (raw) prawns (shrimp), peeled and cleaned
    with tails intact
1 tablespoon fish sauce
1 tablespoon lime juice
200g cooked rice noodles
sliced chilli, coriander (cilantro), Vietnamese mint
    leaves and lime wedges, to serve

Place red chilli coconut paste, coconut cream and stock
into a large saucepan over medium-high heat and bring
to a simmer. Add pumpkin, cover and cook for 15 minutes
or until just tender.
    Add prawns and cook for 3–4 minutes or until cooked
through. Add fish sauce and lime juice and stir through.
    Divide noodles between serving bowls and ladle the
soup over the top. Serve with chilli, coriander, mint
and lime. SERVES 4

chilli coconut chicken stir-fry

500g chicken breast fillets, trimmed and sliced
½ cup (140g) red chilli coconut paste (see *recipe* p198)
¼ cup (60ml) vegetable oil
2 onions, thickly sliced
16 asparagus stalks, trimmed and halved lengthways
300g snake beans, trimmed and halved
250g bok choy, trimmed
sliced chilli, Thai basil leaves, cooked brown basmati
    rice, to serve

Mix the chicken and half the red chilli coconut paste
in a bowl to combine.
    Heat a large frying pan or wok over medium-high heat.
Add 1 tablespoon oil and cook the chicken for 6 minutes,
until golden and cooked through. Remove from the pan.
    Return pan to medium-high heat. Add remaining oil,
remaining red chilli coconut paste and onion and cook for
3–4 minutes. Add asparagus, beans and bok choy and cook
for 3–4 minutes. Return chicken to the pan and cook for
2 minutes or until heated through.
    Top the chicken with the chilli and Thai basil leaves
and serve with rice. SERVES 4

baked fish cakes with gin mayo

500g skinless firm white fish fillet
1 cup (140g) cooked quinoa
½ cup (140g) red chilli coconut paste (see *recipe* p198)
2 tablespoons chopped coriander (cilantro) leaves
sea salt flakes
1 egg white
vegetable oil, for brushing
8 small flatbreads
2 Lebanese cucumbers, thinly sliced
5 cups (125g) mixed salad leaves
lime wedges, to serve
gin mayo
⅔ cup (200g) whole egg mayonnaise
1 tablespoon gin

Preheat oven grill (broiler) to high.
    To make the fish cakes, finely chop the fish and place
in a bowl with the quinoa, red chilli coconut paste,
coriander, sea salt and egg white. Mix to combine.
    Shape ¼ cupfuls of the fish mixture into 12 patties and
place on a baking tray lined with non-stick baking paper.
Brush with oil and grill for 3–4 minutes each side, or until
golden and cooked through.
    To make the gin mayo, mix the mayonnaise and gin
together to combine.
    Place flatbreads on serving plates and top with
cucumber, salad leaves, gin mayo and fish cakes. Serve
with a squeeze of lime. SERVES 4 (MAKES 12 FISH CAKES)

Swap the fish for chicken mince for a simple change-up.

baked fish cakes with gin mayo

RED CHILLI COCONUT PASTE
Choose Your Own *adventure*

chilli coconut vegetable curry

Heat a large saucepan over medium-high heat. Add **2 tablespoons vegetable oil** and **½ cup (140g) red chilli coconut paste (see *recipe* p198)**. Cook for 4 minutes or until fragrant. Add **750g peeled and chopped orange sweet potato (kumara), 500g cauliflower florets, 2 cups (500ml) coconut milk** and **1½ cups (375ml) vegetable** or **chicken stock**. Cover and simmer for 10 minutes or until the potato is almost tender. Add **200g trimmed and halved green beans** and cook for 4 minutes or until tender. Serve with **coriander (cilantro) leaves, a drizzle of fish sauce** and **lime juice** and **steamed brown rice**. SERVES 4

spiced grilled chicken salad

Spread **3 small chicken breast fillets** generously with **red chilli coconut paste (see *recipe* p198)** and place on a baking tray lined with non-stick paper. Drizzle with **a little vegetable oil.** Cook under a preheated grill (broiler) for 8–10 minutes or until golden and cooked through. Slice the chicken and serve with a salad of **4 cups (500g) shredded green mango** or **green papaya** tossed with **1 cup (16g) mint leaves** and **1 cup (16g) coriander (cilantro) leaves.** Toss salad in a dressing of **2 tablespoons each lime juice and fish sauce** mixed with **1 tablespoon brown sugar**. SERVES 4

chilli coconut salmon skewers

Slice **650g salmon fillets** into large chunks and thread onto metal skewers. Spread the salmon generously with the **red chilli coconut paste (see *recipe* p198).** Cook the skewers under a hot preheated grill (broiler) or on a hot barbecue for 2 minutes each side or until the paste is caramelised and the salmon is cooked to your liking. Serve the skewers with **a squeeze of lime, steamed jasmine rice** and **crunchy steamed greens**. SERVES 4

chilli coconut beef stir-fry

Slice **400g beef fillet or tender steaks** into thin strips. Place a deep frying pan or wok over high heat. Add **2 tablespoons vegetable oil** and **2 sliced onions** and cook for 3 minutes or until slightly charred on the edges. Add **½ cup (140g) red chilli coconut paste (see *recipe* p198)** and cook for 2 minutes or until fragrant. Add the beef and cook for 5 minutes or until the beef is well seared. Toss through **300g trimmed snow peas (mange tout), ½ cup (75g) roasted unsalted cashews** and **½ cup (10g) Thai** or **regular basil leaves**. Serve with **cooked rice noodles**. SERVES 4

Poaching garlic in oil gives you the *most versatile,* SOFT AND SILKY condiment. You get jammy cloves and a rich, *velvety oil*, otherwise known as LIQUID GOLD.

confit garlic

4 whole garlic heads, cloves separated (see p14)
2 cups (500 ml) extra virgin olive oil
3 sprigs lemon thyme
½ tablespoon finely grated lemon rind

Preheat oven to 160°C (325°F). Place the peeled garlic cloves in a deep 20cm (8 inch) ceramic baking dish and flatten out evenly. Add the lemon thyme and lemon rind and cover with oil. Make sure the garlic is fully submerged in the oil, adding more oil if needed.

Cook for 40–45 minutes or until the garlic cloves are soft.

While the garlic and oil are hot, transfer to a sterilised glass jar[+], seal and store in the fridge for up to 2 weeks.

MAKES 2 CUPS (500ML)

+ *To sterilise glass jars, preheat oven to 120°C (250°F). Wash the jars and their lids in soapy water, rinse and place on a baking tray. Place in the oven for 20 minutes. Remove and allow to cool before filling. It is essential to sterilise jars thoroughly and to store confit garlic and oil in the fridge to reduce the risk of foodborne illnesses such as botulism. Garlic is particularly prone to botulism as the bulbs can pick up the bacteria that cause it from the soil. When using the garlic, don't leave the jar out at room temperature for too long.*

For a snack on the run, spread mashed confit garlic on toast with sea salt flakes.

warm garlic and cannellini bean salad

confit garlic ricotta gnocchi

warm garlic and cannellini bean salad

2 tablespoons confit garlic oil (see *recipe* p206)
2 x 400g cans cannellini (white) beans,
** rinsed and drained**
2 tablespoons salted capers, rinsed and drained
6 cloves confit garlic, halved (see *recipe* p206)
2 lemons, cut into cheeks
16 asparagus stalks, trimmed, blanched and
** cut lengthways**
3¼ cups (80g) rocket (arugula) leaves
2 tablespoons pine nuts, toasted
extra virgin olive oil, to serve
sea salt and cracked black pepper

Heat a large non-stick frying pan over medium-high heat.
Add the confit garlic oil, beans and capers and cook for
2–3 minutes, or until the beans are heated through.

Add the confit garlic and gently mix to combine.
Remove from the pan and set aside.

Wipe the pan clean and turn the heat up to high. Add the
lemon cheeks and cook for 2 minutes or until caramelised.

To serve, top white bean mixture with asparagus and
rocket and sprinkle with pine nuts. Drizzle with oil, add
the caramelised lemon cheeks and sprinkle with salt and
pepper. SERVES 4

potato and radicchio salad with garlic dressing

800g kipfler or boiling potatoes, cooked and cooled
1 large radicchio, trimmed, leaves separated
400g poached chicken, sliced
1 cup (180g) seedless grapes, halved
¾ cup (18g) flat-leaf (Italian) parsley leaves
120g blue cheese, broken into large chunks
garlic dressing
10 cloves confit garlic (see *recipe* p206)
¼ cup (60ml) confit garlic oil (see *recipe* p206)
2 tablespoons sherry vinegar
sea salt and cracked black pepper

To make the garlic dressing, place the confit garlic, confit
garlic oil, vinegar, salt and pepper in a small food
processor and process until smooth. Set aside.

To serve, top the potato and radicchio with poached
chicken, grapes, parsley and blue cheese. Drizzle with
the garlic dressing. SERVES 4

confit garlic ricotta gnocchi

8 cloves confit garlic (see *recipe* p206)
1½ cups (360g) fresh ricotta
1 cup (80g) finely grated parmesan, plus extra
** to serve**
2 teaspoons finely grated lemon rind
1 cup (150g) plain (all-purpose) flour, plus extra
** for dusting**
3 eggs, lightly whisked
sea salt and cracked black pepper
180g wild rocket (arugula), to serve
lemon chilli garlic dressing
½ cup (125ml) confit garlic oil (see *recipe* p206)
2 tablespoons lemon juice
1 teaspoon finely grated lemon rind
½ teaspoon chilli flakes

To make the lemon chilli garlic dressing, combine the
confit garlic oil, lemon juice and rind, and chilli flakes.
Set aside.

To make the gnocchi, mash the confit garlic cloves to
form a paste. Place in a bowl with ricotta, parmesan,
lemon rind, flour, eggs, salt and pepper and mix until a
soft and sticky dough forms. Divide dough in half.

Using a sieve, very lightly dust a clean surface with flour
and roll each piece of dough into a 3cm-wide (1¼ inch) log.
Lightly sift a little more flour over each gnocchi log and
slice into 2cm-thick (¾ inch) pieces. Set aside on a lightly
floured tray.

Cook the gnocchi in 2 batches in a large saucepan of
boiling salted water for 2–3 minutes, or until they are firm
and rise to the surface.

To serve, divide the gnocchi and rocket between bowls
and drizzle with lemon chilli garlic dressing and extra
parmesan. SERVES 4

potato and radicchio salad with garlic dressing

CONFIT GARLIC
Choose Your Own *adventure*

confit garlic mac and cheese

Mash **8 cloves confit garlic (see** *recipe* **p206)** until smooth. Cook **400g dried penne** in boiling salted water until al dente. Drain, reserving **¾ cup pasta cooking water** and return pasta to the pan. Add the mashed garlic and **2 tablespoons confit garlic oil (see** *recipe* **p206)** and cook over medium heat for 1 minute. Add **1¼ cups (300g) crème fraîche, 1 tablespoon Dijon mustard, the reserved pasta water, 1 cup each grated gruyère and parmesan**, and **sea salt and cracked black pepper.** Cook, stirring for 2 minutes or until the cheeses have melted to combine. Spoon into bowls and serve. SERVES 4

confit garlic pan greens

Mash **8 cloves confit garlic (see** *recipe* **p206)** until smooth. Mix the garlic with **½ cup (120g) sour cream** and set aside. Heat a large frying pan over medium-high heat. Add **2 tablespoons confit garlic oil (see** *recipe* **p206), 1 tablespoon finely grated lemon rind, 1 tablespoon grated fresh horseradish, 8 cups (200g) baby spinach leaves, 4 cups (140g) finely shredded kale leaves, ½ cup (26g) chopped parsley leaves, sea salt** and **cracked black pepper**, and cook for 3–4 minutes or until wilted. Serve the greens on **slices of chargrilled rye or toasted sourdough** topped with the **garlic sour cream.** SERVES 4

confit garlic pasta

Mash **10 cloves confit garlic (see** *recipe* **p206)** until smooth. Cook **400g dried spaghetti** in boiling salted water until al dente. Drain, reserving **¼ cup pasta cooking water**. Return pasta to the pan with the pasta cooking water. Stir the garlic through the hot pasta with **¼ cup confit garlic oil (see** *recipe* **p206), salt and pepper.** Divide between serving bowls, top generously with **grated parmesan** and serve. SERVES 4

confit garlic steak sandwich

Cook **500g beef steak** of your choice until cooked to your liking. Thinly slice steak and sprinkle with **salt and pepper.** Halve **4 bread rolls**. Mash **8 cloves confit garlic (see** *recipe* **p206)** until smooth and mix with **½ cup (150g) whole egg mayonnaise** and **2 tablespoons chopped basil leaves** to combine. Spread the garlic mayo over the bread rolls and top with the sliced steak, **sliced fresh tomato** and **rocket (arugula) leaves**, and serve. SERVES 4

This paste should come with an *addiction warning!* The **PERFECT BALANCE** of *salty-zingy-yum*, it will soon become a part of your **NEW BFF CIRCLE**.

lime and lemongrass paste

7 stalks lemongrass, white parts only, chopped
12 cloves garlic, chopped
100g ginger, peeled and chopped
16 kaffir lime leaves, chopped
1 brown onion, chopped
½ cup (125ml) vegetable oil
1 cup (220g) raw caster (superfine) sugar
½ cup (125ml) rice wine vinegar
½ cup (125ml) fish sauce
2 tablespoons finely grated lime rind
¼ cup (60ml) lime juice
1 teaspoon sea salt flakes or ¼ teaspoon table salt

Place lemongrass, garlic, ginger, kaffir lime leaves, onion and oil in a food processor and process until very finely chopped.

Heat a medium frying pan over medium heat. Add the lemongrass paste and cook, stirring occasionally, for 6–7 minutes or until the mixture has softened. Add sugar, vinegar, fish sauce, lime rind and juice, and sea salt. Reduce heat to medium-low and simmer for 10–12 minutes, stirring occasionally, until lightly browned and caramelised.

You can keep this paste in an airtight container in the fridge for up to 8 weeks. **MAKES 2⅔ CUPS (800G)**

This paste adds a great zesty kick to everything that crosses its path.

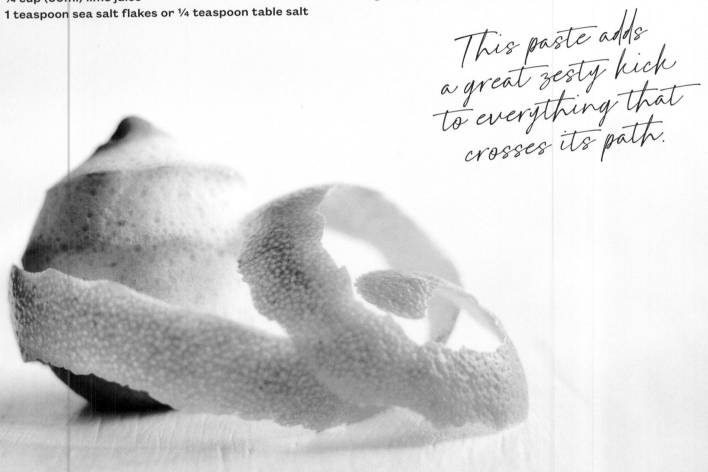

lime and lemongrass grilled salmon fillet with asian greens

lime and lemongrass tofu with charred snap peas

lime and lemongrass grilled salmon fillet with asian greens

450g gai lan (Chinese broccoli), trimmed
450g bok choy, trimmed and halved
4 x 150g salmon fillets, skin removed
½ cup (150g) lime and lemongrass paste
   (see *recipe* p214)
2 tablespoons vegetable oil
cooked brown rice, thinly sliced kaffir lime leaves,
   coriander (cilantro) leaves and lime wedges, to serve

Preheat oven grill (broiler) to high.

Place the gai lan and bok choy in a bowl and cover with boiling water. Allow to stand for 30 seconds, then drain.

Place the greens in 4 piles on a baking tray lined with non-stick baking paper and top with the salmon. Spread salmon and greens with the lime and lemongrass paste, drizzle with oil and grill for 3–4 minutes or until the salmon is cooked to your liking.

Serve the salmon and greens bundles with brown rice, kaffir lime, coriander and lime wedges. **SERVES 4**

lime and lemongrass tofu with charred snap peas

600g sugar snap peas, trimmed
1 tablespoon vegetable oil
800g firm tofu, drained and sliced into 7cm x 2cm
   (2¾ inch x ¾ inch) rectangles
4 green onions (scallions), sliced
½ cup (150g) lime and lemongrass paste
   (see *recipe* p214)
cooked rice noodles, coriander (cilantro) leaves,
   roasted cashews and lime wedges, to serve

Heat a large frying pan or wok over high heat.

Toss the sugar snap peas and oil in a bowl to coat. Add the sugar snaps to the hot pan and cook for 3–4 minutes, turning occasionally, until slightly charred. Remove from the pan and set aside.

Add the tofu, green onion and lime and lemongrass paste and cook for 3 minutes or until the paste is caramelised and the tofu is heated through. Return the sugar snaps to the pan and toss to combine.

Serve the sugar snap peas and tofu with noodles, coriander, cashews and lime wedges. **SERVES 4**

lime and lemongrass chicken larb

500g chicken mince
½ cup (150g) lime and lemongrass paste
   (see *recipe* p214)
2 tablespoons vegetable oil
1 tablespoon fish sauce
2 baby cos (romaine) lettuce, leaves separated
   (about 12 leaves)
Thai basil, mint and coriander (cilantro) leaves,
   to serve
pickled carrot
½ cup (125ml) rice wine vinegar
1 tablespoon raw caster (superfine) sugar
1 long red chilli, finely chopped
3 large carrots, peeled and shredded using a
   julienne peeler

To make the pickled carrot, mix the rice wine vinegar, sugar and chilli in a bowl until the sugar has dissolved. Add the carrots and allow to stand for 3–5 minutes or until they soften slightly. Set aside.

In a large bowl, mix the chicken mince and lime and lemongrass paste together until combined.

Heat a large frying pan or wok over high heat. Add the oil and chicken mixture and cook for 6–8 minutes or until the chicken is a light golden brown and is cooked through. Add the fish sauce and mix to combine.

To serve, top the cos lettuce cups with the lime and lemongrass chicken, pickled carrot, basil, mint and coriander leaves. **SERVES 4**

Swap chicken mince for pork mince, chopped tofu or plant-based mince.

lime and lemongrass chicken larb

LIME AND LEMONGRASS PASTE
Choose Your Own *adventure*

lime and lemongrass noodles

Heat a large wok or frying pan over medium-high heat. Add **2 tablespoons vegetable oil** and **½ cup (150g) lime and lemongrass paste (see *recipe* p214)** and cook for 2 minutes. Add **500g chopped firm tofu** or **3 sliced chicken breast fillets** to the pan and cook for 5 minutes or until browned and cooked through. Add **300g trimmed snow peas (mange tout)**, **550g cooked rice noodles** and stir until heated through. Serve with **a little drizzle of fish sauce**, **a squeeze of fresh lime juice** and **a sprinkle of roasted unsalted cashews**. SERVES 4

lime and lemongrass prawn skewers

Thread **24 large cleaned green (raw) prawns (shrimp)** onto 8 metal skewers. Spread the prawns generously with **lime and lemongrass paste (see *recipe* p214)**. Cook under a hot preheated grill (broiler) for 3 minutes each side or until the prawns are cooked through. Serve the prawns with **steamed jasmine rice**, **steamed greens** and **lime wedges**. SERVES 4

lime and lemongrass pork burgers

Combine **⅓ cup (100g) lime and lemongrass paste (see *recipe* p214)** with **500g pork, chicken or beef mince** and **½ cup (30g) panko breadcrumbs** and mix together. Shape into 4 large patties. Heat oil in a large non-stick frying pan and cook patties for 6 minutes each side or until cooked through. To serve, spread burger buns with **sriracha hot chilli sauce** and **mayonnaise** and top with the patties, **shredded carrot**, **coriander (cilantro) leaves** and **a squeeze of fresh lime**. SERVES 4

simple grilled lime and lemongrass chicken

Place **4 small chicken breast fillets** on a baking tray. Spread generously with **lime and lemongrass paste (see *recipe* p214)** and **drizzle with a little oil**. Cook under a hot preheated grill (broiler) for 8–10 minutes or until the chicken is just cooked through. To serve, slice the chicken and toss through **3 shredded Lebanese cucumbers** and **¾ cups (42g) shredded mint leaves**. SERVES 4

Loaded with SALTY-SWEET completely *addictive flavour*, this MISO MARINADE will elevate the most *humble ingredients* to rock star status.

sticky miso marinade

1 cup (250g) white (shiro) miso paste
¼ cup (60g) finely grated ginger
¼ cup (60ml) sesame oil
¾ cup (180ml) mirin
¼ cup (60ml) rice wine vinegar
½ cup (125ml) pure maple syrup

Place the white miso paste, ginger, sesame oil, mirin, rice wine vinegar and maple syrup in a bowl and mix to combine.

You can keep this paste in an airtight container in the fridge for up to 8 weeks. **MAKES 2¾ CUP (700ML)**

Miso pastes vary in flavour. The lighter the paste, the milder the flavour.

miso chicken caesar salad

sticky miso beef poke bowl

miso chicken caesar salad

6 x 125g chicken thigh fillets, trimmed
⅓ cup (80ml) sticky miso marinade (see *recipe* p222)
2 baby cos (romaine) lettuce, trimmed
2½ cups (90g) firmly packed shredded kale leaves
chopped wasabi peas and shaved parmesan, to serve
dressing
¾ cup (180ml) sticky miso marinade (see *recipe* p222)
½ cup (125ml) water
½ cup (140g) hulled tahini

Preheat oven grill (broiler) to high.

Toss the chicken in the sticky miso marinade and place on a baking tray lined with non-stick baking paper. Grill for 15 minutes or until golden and cooked through. Cool slightly, then slice.

To make the dressing, mix the sticky miso marinade, water and tahini in a bowl. Combine the cos, kale and half of the dressing in a bowl and toss to coat.

To serve, top the cos and kale leaves with the chicken. Spoon the remaining dressing over the top and sprinkle with wasabi peas and parmesan. **SERVES 4**

seared miso tofu with pickled soba noodle salad

600g firm silken tofu, cut into 2cm (¾ inch) slices
½ cup (125ml) sticky miso marinade (see *recipe* p222)
black sesame seeds and baby shiso leaves, to serve
pickled soba noodle salad
270g dried soba noodles, cooked, drained and
    refreshed under cold water
3 carrots, peeled and shredded using a julienne peeler
3 Lebanese cucumbers, shredded using a julienne peeler
3 green onions (scallions), finely sliced
⅓ cup (80ml) brown rice vinegar
2 tablespoons mirin
⅓ cup (80ml) sticky miso marinade (see *recipe* p222)

Preheat oven grill (broiler) to high.

Place the tofu on a baking tray lined with non-stick baking paper, top with the miso marinade and set aside.

To make the pickled soba noodle salad, combine the noodles, carrot, cucumber and green onions. Combine the vinegar, mirin and miso marinade and pour over the salad.

Grill the tofu for 12 minutes or until golden.

Serve the noodle salad topped with the tofu, sesame seeds and shiso leaves. **SERVES 4**

sticky miso beef poke bowl

500g beef eye fillet
extra virgin olive oil, for drizzling
sea salt and cracked black pepper
¾ cup (180ml) sticky miso marinade (see *recipe* p222)
½ cup (125ml) water
1 tablespoon mirin
poke bowl
4 cups (660g) cooked brown rice
1 cup (140g) frozen shelled edamame beans, blanched
4 watermelon radishes, thinly sliced
2 Lebanese cucumbers, thinly sliced
2 avocados, sliced into wedges
4 green onions (scallions), finely sliced
shredded nori sheets and sesame seeds, to serve

Preheat oven to 200°C (400°F).

Drizzle the beef with oil and sprinkle with salt and pepper. Heat an ovenproof non-stick frying pan over high heat. Sear the beef for 2 minutes on all sides until evenly browned. Remove the pan from the heat and spoon the sticky miso marinade over the beef. Transfer the pan to the oven and roast for 5 minutes, then turn beef over and cook for a further 5–7 minutes or until cooked to your liking[+]. Transfer beef to a plate and rest for 4–5 minutes. Slice into thin pieces.

Return the pan and remaining juices to the heat and bring to the boil. Reduce heat to medium, add water and mirin and cook for 3–5 minutes, stirring occasionally or until the sauce starts to thicken.

To serve, divide the rice, edamame, radish, cucumber, avocado, green onions, shredded nori, beef and sesame seeds between serving bowls and drizzle with the warm sauce. **SERVES 4**

+ *For medium rare, we recommend cooking for 5 minutes, turning and cooking for a further 5–7 minutes. For medium to well done, we recommend cooking for 7 minutes, turning and cooking for a further 7 minutes.*

seared miso tofu with pickled soba noodle salad

STICKY MISO MARINADE
Choose Your Own *adventure*

sticky miso stir-fried greens

Heat a large frying pan or wok over high heat. Add **1 tablespoon sesame oil, 200g trimmed snow peas (mange tout), 200g trimmed baby green beans** and **300g trimmed and halved asparagus**. Cook, stirring for 3 minutes, then add **½ cup (125ml) sticky miso marinade (see *recipe* p222)** and stir for another 2 minutes or until the miso marinade has thickened and is caramelised. Serve as a side dish or tossed through **cooked noodles** or with **cooked brown rice**. SERVES 4

sticky miso pumpkin

Preheat oven to 220°C (425°F). Place **1.2kg of large pumpkin chunks** into a baking dish lined with non-stick baking paper. Spoon **¾ cup (180ml) sticky miso marinade (see *recipe* p222)** over the pumpkin and toss to coat. Bake for 35–40 minutes or until the pumpkin is soft and caramelised. Sprinkle with **sesame seeds** and **sliced green onions (scallions)** to serve. SERVES 4

sticky miso udon

Place **550g fresh udon noodles** into a bowl and cover with boiling water. Allow to stand for 5 minutes, then drain. Heat a large frying pan or wok over medium-high heat. Add the noodles, **1 tablespoon vegetable oil, ½ cup (125ml) sticky miso marinade (see *recipe* p222)** and **4 sliced green onions (scallions)** and cook, stirring for 6 minutes or until the noodles are golden and caramelised. Serve sprinkled with **black sesame seeds** or **shredded nori sheets** as a side dish. SERVES 4

sticky miso cod

Spread **4 x 150g pieces cod** generously with the **sticky miso marinade (see *recipe* p222)**. Cook the fish under a very hot preheated grill (broiler) until the sticky miso is a deep golden brown colour and the fish is cooked through. Serve the sticky miso cod with **steamed rice, pickled ginger** and **lime wedges**. SERVES 4

Calling on a BOUNTY OF SPICES and aromats,
with yoghurt to *tenderise proteins*, this CURRY PASTE
is *the superstar* your FREEZER NEEDS.

tikka curry paste

2 cups (560g) plain thick yoghurt
6 cloves garlic, crushed
2 tablespoons (40g) finely grated ginger
½ tablespoon garam masala
½ tablespoon ground turmeric
½ tablespoon ground cumin
½ tablespoon ground coriander (cilantro) seeds
1 teaspoon sea salt flakes
1 teaspoon sweet smoked paprika
½ teaspoon chilli powder

Place the yoghurt, garlic, ginger, garam masala, turmeric, cumin, coriander seeds, salt, paprika and chilli powder in a bowl and mix to combine.

Spoon the paste into ice cube trays or small containers and freeze until solid. Once solid, place in an airtight container and store in the freezer until needed.

You can keep this paste in an airtight container in the freezer for up to 8 weeks. **MAKES 2 CUPS (500G)**

What could be easier than defrosting a few cubes of this curry paste when you need it?

230

grilled chicken tikka with roti and sumac yoghurt

SCAN THIS CODE FOR RECIPE VIDEO

baked cauliflower, chickpea and lentil tikka

grilled chicken tikka with roti and sumac yoghurt

6 x 125g chicken thigh fillets, trimmed and halved
½ cup (125g) tikka curry paste (see *recipe* p230)
sea salt and cracked black pepper
2 tablespoons extra virgin olive oil
2 Lebanese cucumbers, thinly sliced
store-bought roti, plain thick yoghurt sprinkled
**   with sumac and mint leaves, to serve**

Preheat oven grill (broiler) to high.

In a large bowl, place the chicken, tikka curry paste, salt and pepper and mix until the chicken is well coated.

Place the chicken on a baking tray lined with non-stick baking paper and drizzle with oil. Grill for 15 minutes or until a deep golden colour and cooked through.

Top the roti with chicken and serve with cucumber, sumac yoghurt and mint. **SERVES 4**

baked cauliflower, chickpea and lentil tikka

1 cauliflower, trimmed and cut into florets
1 x 400g can lentils, rinsed and drained
1 x 400g can chickpeas (garbanzo beans),
**   rinsed and drained**
2 brown onions, sliced
1½ cups (375g) tikka curry paste (see *recipe* p230)
sea salt and cracked black pepper
400g paneer, cut into large pieces
6 sprigs curry leaves
¼ cup (60ml) extra virgin olive oil
baby spinach leaves, coriander (cilantro) leaves,
**   lemon wedges and plain thick yoghurt, to serve**

Preheat oven to 220°C (425°F).

Place the cauliflower, lentils, chickpeas, onion and tikka curry paste in a large bowl and mix until well coated. Sprinkle with salt and pepper.

Place the cauliflower mixture onto a large baking tray lined with non-stick baking paper and top with paneer and curry sprigs. Drizzle with oil and bake for 45–55 minutes, stirring occasionally, until golden and crispy.

Serve the cauliflower and paneer with spinach and coriander leaves, lemon wedges and yoghurt. **SERVES 4**

grilled tikka lamb cutlets with pear and fennel salad

12 lamb cutlets, trimmed
¾ cup (185g) tikka curry paste (see *recipe* p230)
micro mint or mint leaves and red veined sorrel
**   leaves, to serve**
extra virgin olive oil, for drizzling
pear and fennel salad
2 tablespoons extra virgin olive oil
2 tablespoons apple cider vinegar
1 tablespoon honey
2 fennels, thinly sliced using a mandoline
2 firm green or brown pears, thinly sliced using
**   a mandoline**

Combine the lamb cutlets and tikka curry paste and mix to coat. Allow to stand at room temperature for 10 minutes.

Preheat oven grill (broiler) to high.

Place the lamb cutlets on a baking tray lined with non-stick baking paper, drizzle with oil and grill for 3–4 minutes each side or until lightly charred and cooked to your liking.

To make the pear and fennel salad, mix the oil, vinegar and honey in a bowl to combine. Add the fennel and pear and gently toss to coat.

Serve the lamb cutlets with the pear and fennel salad, mint and red veined sorrel. **SERVES 4**

A cool salad or yoghurt teams well with the warm tones in this curry paste.

grilled tikka lamb cutlets with pear and fennel salad

TIKKA CURRY PASTE
Choose Your Own *adventure*

tikka grilled salmon

Slice **650g salmon fillet**, **ocean trout fillet** or **thick firm white fish fillet** into large chunks and thread onto metal skewers. Coat generously with the **tikka curry paste (see *recipe* p230)** and drizzle with **vegetable oil.** Place on a baking tray lined with non-stick paper and grill under a hot preheated grill (broiler) for 6–7 minutes or until the tikka paste is golden and the fish is cooked. Serve with **warm flatbreads** and **plain thick yoghurt** that has been mixed with **chopped cucumber** and **fresh mint.** SERVES 4

tikka roast potatoes

Boil **1kg new potatoes** in salted water until just tender and drain. Slice the potatoes in half and place on a baking tray lined with non-stick baking paper. Top with **¾ cup (185g) tikka curry paste (see *recipe* p230)** and toss to coat. **Drizzle with vegetable oil** and bake in a preheated 220°C (425°F) oven for 30 minutes or until golden. Sprinkle with **coriander (cilantro) leaves** and **sea salt**, to serve. SERVES 4

tikka flat-roast chicken

Preheat oven to 220°C (425°F). Cut away the backbone from a **1.2kg whole chicken** and discard. Place the butterfied chicken on a baking tray lined with non-stick baking paper, skin-side up. Spread the chicken with **¾ cup (185g) tikka curry paste (see *recipe* p230)** and drizzle with **vegetable oil.** Bake for 45–60 minutes (depending on the size of your chicken) or until golden and cooked through. Serve the chicken with a simple **tomato and mint salad.** SERVES 4

tikka lamb leg

Preheat oven to 240°C (475°F). Take a trimmed **1kg flattened boneless leg of lamb** and make deep slashes across the meat. Place lamb in a baking dish and coat generously with **tikka curry paste (see *recipe* p230).** Drizzle with vegetable oil and bake for 30 minutes or until the lamb is cooked to your liking. To serve, slice the lamb thinly and place on **flatbreads** with **store-bought sweet pickled onions** and **mango chutney.** SERVES 4

Flavour Starters

sweet

Smooth and *super-glossy,* this coconut-kissed
GOLDEN GODDESS is powered with *better-for-you*
stuff to ENRICH EVERYTHING in its path.

coconut caramel

2 cups (500ml) coconut cream
1½ cups (225g) coconut sugar
2 teaspoons vanilla extract

Place the coconut cream, sugar and vanilla in a large non-stick frying pan over high heat and stir for 2 minutes, until the sugar dissolves and the mixture is boiling.

Cook caramel over medium-high heat, stirring occasionally, paying close attention as the caramel can stick to the bottom of the pan. Continue stirring for 8–10 minutes or until the caramel has thickened and reduced to 400ml when measured in a heatproof jug. It should leave a trail when you run your spoon or spatula through it.

Allow to cool slightly before pouring into sterilised jars or clean glass storage containers. Refrigerate for up to 8 weeks. **MAKES 400ML**

coconut tahini caramel slice

caramel basque burnt cheesecake

caramel basque burnt cheesecake

750g cream cheese, chopped and softened
1½ cups (225g) coconut sugar or firmly packed
  brown sugar
4 large eggs
1½ cups (375ml) double (thick) cream
1 teaspoon vanilla bean paste
1½ tablespoons plain (all-purpose) flour or rice flour
coconut caramel (see *recipe* **p240), to serve**

Preheat oven to 220°C (425°F). Line a 22cm (8½ inch) springform tin or a 22cm (8½ inch) ovenproof frying pan with 3 large pieces of overlapping non-stick baking paper, ensuring the paper extends above the rim+.

Place the cheese and sugar into the bowl of an electric mixer. Using the whisk attachment, beat for 8–10 minutes, until soft peaks form. Add eggs one at a time, beating after each addition, until combined.

Add cream and vanilla and beat until just combined. Sift flour over the cream and beat on low until just combined. Pour into the prepared tin and bake for 15 minutes, then rotate cake and bake for a further 10–15 minutes. The cheesecake should rise up like a soufflé and caramelise, almost burning on top, but still have a strong wobble in the middle.

Once out of the oven, leave cheesecake to cool for 1 hour (it will sink a bit), then refrigerate until chilled. Serve with a drizzle of coconut caramel. **SERVES 10**
+ *The triple layer of baking paper that extends high above the tin protects the sides from burning.*

coconut caramel tahini slice

2 cups (240g) almond meal (ground almonds)
½ cup (75g) coconut sugar
⅔ cup (180g) hulled tahini
⅓ cup (80ml) pure maple syrup
2 teaspoons vanilla extract
2½ tablespoons cornflour (cornstarch)
400ml (1¾ cups) cooled coconut caramel (see
  recipe p240)
chocolate topping
125g dark (70% cocoa) chocolate, chopped
3 teaspoons vegetable oil

Preheat oven to 160°C (325°F). Line a 20cm (8 inch) square cake tin with non-stick baking paper.

Place the almond meal, sugar, tahini, maple syrup and vanilla in a bowl and mix to combine.

Using the back of a spoon, press mixture into the prepared tin and bake for 25–30 minutes or until a deep golden colour.

Place the cornflour and ⅓ cup of the coconut caramel into a bowl and whisk to combine. Place in a non-stick frying pan with the remaining coconut caramel, stir well and cook over medium-high heat for 5 minutes, stirring continuously, until the caramel is very thick.

Pour the coconut caramel over the base mixture, return to the oven and cook for 20 minutes. Allow to stand for 30 minutes, until cooled slightly.

To make the chocolate topping, place the chocolate and oil in a heatproof bowl over a saucepan of simmering water and stir until melted and smooth. Pour the chocolate over the coconut caramel mixture and spread evenly. Refrigerate for 4 hours, or until firm.

Using a warm knife, cut into slices or squares to serve. Store in an airtight container in the fridge. **MAKES 18 BARS**

coconut caramel tart

2 tablespoons sunflower seeds
2 tablespoons pepitas (pumpkin seeds)
1 tablespoon hemp seeds (optional)
2 tablespoons coconut flour
6 soft fresh dates, pitted
1 teaspoon vanilla extract
¼ cup (60g) cashew, almond or peanut butter
2½ tablespoons cornflour (cornstarch)
400ml (1¾ cups) cooled coconut caramel (see
  recipe p240)
100g dark (70% cocoa) chocolate, melted

To make the tart shell, place the sunflower seeds and pepitas in a food processor and process until a fine crumb. Add the hemp seeds, coconut flour, dates, vanilla and nut butter and process until combined. Press the mixture into an 18cm (7 inch) fluted tart tin and set aside.

Place the cornflour and ⅓ cup of the coconut caramel into a bowl and whisk to combine. Place in a non-stick frying pan with the remaining coconut caramel, stir well and cook over medium-high heat for 5 minutes, stirring continuously, until the caramel is very thick.

Pour the coconut caramel into the tart shell and refrigerate for 2–3 hours, until set.

Drizzle with melted dark chocolate and serve. **SERVES 6-8**
+ *Keep the tart in an airtight container in the fridge for up to 2 weeks.*

coconut caramel tart

COCONUT CARAMEL
Choose Your Own *adventure*

caramel amaretti parfait

Whisk together **¾ cup (185ml) mascarpone** with **1 cup (250ml) single (pouring) cream**, **¼ cup (60ml) coconut caramel (see *recipe* p240)** and **1 teaspoon vanilla extract** until light and fluffy. Lightly crush **32 small store-bought amaretti biscuits** and place half into the base of 4 serving glasses or bowls. Top with generous spoonfuls of the whipped mascarpone and spoon some of the **coconut caramel** over the top. Repeat the layers and serve. **SERVES 4**

caramel buckwheat pancakes

Place **¾ cup (120g) buckwheat flour**, **¾ cup (90g) plain (all-purpose) wholemeal (whole-wheat) spelt flour**, **3 teaspoons baking powder**, **1 egg**, **1 tablespoon light-flavoured extra virgin olive oil**, **2 tablespoons coconut sugar**, **1 cup (250ml) milk** and **¼ cup (60ml) coconut caramel (see *recipe* p240)** in a blender and blend until smooth. Cook ⅓ cupfuls of the pancake mixture in a non-stick frying pan until puffed and golden. Serve with **extra coconut caramel (see *recipe* p240)** and **sliced fruit**. **SERVES 4**

coconut caramel breakfast smoothie

Place **3 cups (750ml) coconut or nut milk**, **4 ice cubes**, **¼ cup (60ml) coconut caramel (see *recipe* p240)**, **1 tablespoon hemp seeds**, **2 tablespoons cashews** and **1 tablespoon rolled oats** in a blender and blend until smooth. Pour smoothie into glasses and serve. **SERVES 2**

coconut yoghurt and caramel sundaes

Divide **2 cups (560g) plain thick coconut yoghurt** between bowls or serving glasses. Top with **⅓ cup (35g) toasted chopped walnuts or pecans** and **1 finely chopped apple, pear or 1½ cups mixed berries**. Spoon **coconut caramel (see *recipe* p240)** over the top of the sundaes and serve. **SERVES 4**

This dark, rich syrup will PERK UP anything and anyone it meets! Use it to add *delicious depth* of flavour to drinks, sweets and BAKED TREATS.

dark chocolate espresso syrup

200g dark (70% cocoa) chocolate, finely chopped
½ cup (125ml) freshly brewed espresso
⅓ cup (80ml) single (pouring) cream, warmed

Place the chocolate, espresso and cream in a medium heatproof bowl over a saucepan of simmering water (the bowl shouldn't touch the water) and stir for 2–3 minutes or until smooth.

Allow to cool slightly before pouring into sterilised jars or clean glass storage containers. Refrigerate for up to 2–3 weeks. **MAKES 300ML**

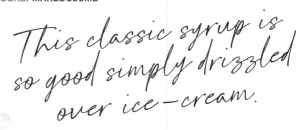

This classic syrup is so good simply drizzled over ice-cream.

simple almond cakes with dark chocolate espresso syrup

dark chocolate espresso semifreddo

simple almond cakes
with dark chocolate espresso syrup

1 cup (240g) firmly packed brown sugar
4 eggs
¼ cup (60ml) light-flavoured extra virgin olive oil
¼ cup (60ml) milk or nut milk
3 cups (360g) almond meal (ground almonds)
1 teaspoon baking powder
dark chocolate espresso syrup (see *recipe* p248),
   to serve

Preheat oven to 160°C (325°F). Grease 6 x 1-cup-capacity
(250ml) muffin tins.

Place the sugar, eggs, oil and milk in a large bowl and
whisk to combine. Add the almond meal and baking
powder and whisk until smooth.

Pour the mixture into the muffin tins and bake for
25–30 minutes or until golden and cooked when tested
with a skewer. Allow to cool in the tins for 10 minutes.

Remove the cakes from the tins and place on a cake
stand or plate. Drizzle with dark chocolate espresso
syrup to serve. **SERVES 6**

dark chocolate espresso semifreddo

¾ cup (180ml) dark chocolate espresso syrup
   (see *recipe* p248)
3 eggs
2 egg yolks
2 tablespoons cooled freshly brewed espresso
1 teaspoon vanilla extract
1 cup (220g) raw caster (superfine) sugar
2 cups (500ml) single (pouring) cream

Line an 8-cup (2-litre) capacity 25cm x 10cm (10 inch x
4 inch) metal loaf tin with non-stick baking paper.

Add the dark chocolate espresso syrup to the base
and freeze for 20 minutes.

Meanwhile, to make the semifreddo, place the eggs,
yolks, cooled espresso, vanilla and sugar in a heatproof
bowl. Place over a saucepan of simmering water and beat
for 6–8 minutes with a whisk, until thick and pale. Remove
from the heat and allow to cool slightly.

Whisk the cream until stiff peaks form. Add cream and
gently fold through.

Pour the semifreddo mixture over the set dark
chocolate espresso and freeze for 6 hours or until firm.
SERVES 8–10

dark chocolate espresso tiramisu

¼ cup (60ml) coffee liqueur
2½ tablespoons freshly brewed espresso
1 tablespoon pure maple syrup
12 store-bought sponge finger biscuits
¾ cup (180ml) dark chocolate espresso syrup
   (see *recipe* p248), to serve
ricotta filling
1½ cups (360g) fresh ricotta
¾ cup (180ml) single (pouring) cream
2 teaspoons vanilla extract
¼ cup (55g) raw caster (superfine) sugar

To make the ricotta filling, place the ricotta, cream,
vanilla and sugar into a food processor and process
for 3–4 minutes or until light and fluffy.

To assemble, place the coffee liqueur, espresso
and maple syrup in a bowl and mix to combine. Soak both
sides of the biscuits in the espresso liquid for 5 seconds
and place on serving plates.

Top with the ricotta filling and dark chocolate espresso
syrup and serve. **SERVES 4**

No-fuss desserts turn into showstoppers with this rich and glossy syrup.

dark chocolate espresso tiramisu

DARK CHOC ESPRESSO
Choose Your Own *adventure*

boozy chocolate espresso trifle

Line a 6-cup (1.5 litre) capacity dish with **thick slices of store-bought sponge cake**. Spoon **2 tablespoons coffee liqueur** over the top, and then generous spoonfuls of **dark chocolate espresso syrup (see *recipe* p248)**. Whisk together **1 cup mascarpone, 1 cup (250ml) single (pouring) cream** and **2 tablespoons icing (confectioner's sugar)** until light and fluffy. Spoon half this mixture over the chocolate espresso layer and repeat with remaining ingredients. Finish with **dark chocolate espresso syrup** and chill for 1 hour before serving. **SERVES 6**

chocolate espresso eton mess

Lightly crush **4 large store-bought meringues** into large pieces. Place the meringue into 4 serving glasses or bowls. Place **1 cup (250ml) double (thick) cream, 2 teaspoons vanilla bean paste** and **2 tablespoons icing (confectioner's) sugar** in a bowl and whisk together until the cream is light and fluffy. Spoon the whipped vanilla cream over the meringues and top with generous spoonfuls of **dark chocolate espresso syrup (see *recipe* p248)** before serving. **SERVES 4**

affogato ice-cream sundae

Place **scoops of vanilla ice-cream** into serving bowls or glasses. Pour **½ tablespoon coffee or nut-based liqueur of your choice** over the ice-cream. Top with a drizzle of the **dark chocolate espresso syrup (see *recipe* p248)** and serve. **SERVES 4**

toasted marshmallow mocha

Place **2 tablespoons dark chocolate espresso syrup (see *recipe* p248)** into each mug and top with **hot milk or nut milk**. Stir to combine. Place **6 marshmallows** on a baking tray lined with non-stick baking paper and grill under a preheated oven grill (broiler) for 1 minute or until golden. Place toasted marshmallows on top of the drinks and serve. **SERVES 2**

Glossary *and* Index

agave syrup

Agave syrup is the nectar of the agave succulent and has a mild, neutral sweetness. It's often used in place of sugar, maple syrup or honey. It's available from the health food aisle of supermarkets as light or dark agave. Light agave syrup has a milder flavour.

almond butter

This paste is made from ground almonds and is available at most supermarkets and health food stores. It's a popular alternative to peanut butter for those with peanut allergies (always check the label). Sometimes sold as 'spreads', the nut butters called for in this book are all-natural with no additives.

almond meal (ground almonds)

Almond meal is available from most supermarkets. Take care not to confuse it with almond flour, which has a much finer texture. Make your own almond meal by processing whole almonds to a meal in a food processor – 125g (4½ oz) almonds should give 1 cup of almond meal.

baking powder

A raising agent used in baking, consisting of bicarbonate of soda and/or cream of tartar. Most are gluten free (check the label). Baking powder that's kept beyond its use-by date can lose effectiveness.

bicarbonate of (baking) soda

Also known as baking soda, bicarbonate of soda (sodium bicarbonate) is an alkaline powder used to help leaven baked goods and neutralise acids.

blanching

Blanching is a cooking method used to slightly soften the texture, heighten the colour and enhance the flavour of vegetables. Plunge the ingredient briefly into boiling unsalted water, remove and refresh under cold water. Drain well.

bok choy

A mild-flavoured green vegetable, with fresh crunchy white stems and broad floppy green leaves. It's also known as Chinese chard, Chinese white cabbage or pak choy. It's best trimmed, gently steamed, pan-fried or blanched, then teamed with Asian-style rice and noodle dishes or stir-fries.

broccolini (sprouting broccoli)

Also known as tenderstem broccoli, broccolini is a cross between gai lan (Chinese broccoli) and broccoli. This popular green vegetable has long, thin stems and small florets with a slightly sweet flavour. Sold in bunches, broccolini can be substituted with regular heads of broccoli that have been sliced into slim florets.

butter

Unless it says otherwise in a recipe, butter should be at room temperature for cooking. It should not be half-melted or too soft to handle. We mostly prefer unsalted butter, but use salted if you wish.

buttermilk

Despite its name, buttermilk contains no butter and is lighter than regular cream. It has a light, creamy and slightly tangy flavour, which makes it a healthier creamy addition to pasta sauces and soups. Buttermilk contains cultures and acids that react with raising agents to create carbon dioxide, which helps create light and fluffy cakes, scones and pancakes.

cabbage

chinese

Also known as wombok or napa cabbage, Chinese cabbage is elongated in shape with ribbed green-yellow leaves. It's regularly used in noodle salads and to make kimchi. Find it at Asian grocers and greengrocers.

green

Pale green or white with tightly bound, waxy leaves, these common cabbages are sold whole or halved in supermarkets and are perfect for use in slaws. Choose heads that are firm and unblemished with crisp leaves that are tightly packed.

savoy

The savoy cabbage has green crinkly leaves that are tender and sweeter than other cabbage varieties. It is great in stuffed cabbage recipes, as the leaves are pliable, but it is also eaten raw in salads and coleslaws that call for some crunch. The savoy cabbage is considered a good source of vitamin C and dietary fibre. Find it at supermarkets and greengrocers.

capers

These small green flower buds of the caper bush are packed either in brine or salt. Capers lend their salty-sour intensity to sauces, seafood and pastas. Before using, rinse thoroughly, drain and pat dry.

cashew butter

This paste is made from ground cashews and is available at most supermarkets and health food stores. Often sold as 'spreads', the nut butters called for in this book are all-natural with no additives. Popular in baking recipes, cashew butter often gives cookies and slices a fudgy texture.

cavolo nero (Tuscan kale)

Translated to mean 'black cabbage', this dark leafy vegetable is similar to silverbeet, and is super nutritious. The recipes in this book call for cavolo nero leaves.

cheese

blue

The distinctive blue veins and strong flavour of blue cheeses are achieved by adding a cultured mould. Most have a soft-yet-crumbly texture and acidic taste, which becomes rounded and more mellow with age. Blue cheeses team particularly well with sweet flavours – they're often paired on cheese boards and in salads with quince paste, pear, honey or figs.

buffalo mozzarella

This much-loved variety of fresh Italian mozzarella is made from water buffalo's milk and/or cow's milk. Creamy and salty, it's sold in rounds, or balls, at grocers and delicatessens and is often torn into pieces and scattered over caprese salads, pizza or pasta.

burrata

An Italian stretched-curd cheese made from mozzarella, burrata has a creamy, milky centre. It's best served simply, with something like a tomato or fig salad. It's available from delicatessens, specialty cheese stores, Italian grocery stores and some supermarkets.

feta

A brined white cheese typically bought in blocks that is Greek in origin, feta has a salty, tangy flavour ranging from mild to sharp. Traditionally made using sheep's milk, these days you can find many cow's milk versions. Use it fresh in salads or bake it.

goat's cheese

Goat's milk has a tart flavour, so the cheese made from it, also called chèvre, has a sharp, slightly acidic taste. Immature goat's cheese is mild and creamy and is often labelled goat's curd, which is spreadable. Mature goat's cheese is available in both hard and soft varieties.

haloumi

A firm white Cypriot cheese made from sheep's milk, haloumi has a stringy texture and is usually sold in brine. Slice and pan-fry until golden and heated through for a salty addition to roast vegetables or salads. Buy haloumi at major greengrocers and supermarkets.

parmesan

Italy's favourite hard, granular cheese is made from cow's milk. Parmigiano Reggiano is the best variety, made under strict guidelines in the Emilia-Romagna region and aged for an average of two years. Grana Padano mainly comes from Lombardy and is aged for around 15 months.

ricotta

A creamy, finely grained white cheese. Ricotta means 'recooked' in Italian, a reference to the way the cheese is produced by heating the whey leftover from making other cheese varieties. It's fresh, creamy and low in fat and there is also a reduced-fat version, which is lighter again. Choose fresh ricotta from your delicatessen or supermarket deli.

washed rind cheese

This predominantly soft or semi-soft cheese is known for its strong aroma and crusty red or orange rind, which helps to keep it moist. It works well on a cheese board or as a topping for soups, salads or risottos. Store the cheese in its original wrapper in the refrigerator. You can find washed rind cheeses at the supermarket, deli or at your local cheesemonger.

chia seeds

These ancient seeds come from a flowering plant and are full of protein, omega-3 fatty acids, minerals and fibre. Use the black or white seeds interchangeably. Find them in supermarkets – they're great for smoothies, salads and baking.

chickpeas (garbanzo beans)

A legume native to western Asia and across the Mediterranean, chickpeas are used in soups, stews and are the base ingredient in hummus. Dried chickpeas need soaking before use; buy them canned to skip this step.

chillies

There are more than 200 different types of chillies, or chilli peppers, in the world. Long red or green chillies are generally milder, fruitier and sweeter, while small chillies are much hotter. Remove the membranes and seeds for a milder result.

chipotle in adobo sauce

Chipotle are smoke-dried jalapeño chillies. In adobo sauce, they're sold in cans or jars at supermarkets, specialty grocers and delicatessens. They are popular in Mexican cuisine and also add a great kick when stirred through mayonnaise.

jalapeños

These dark green plump Mexican chillies are known for their medium heat and fresh, bitey flavour. Buy jalapeños sliced in jars, pickled or fresh. Often used in Mexican cuisine, much of their heat is held in the seeds and membranes, which can be removed for a milder intensity.

chinese cooking wine (Shaoxing)

Similar to dry sherry, Shaoxing, or Chinese cooking wine, is a blend of glutinous rice, millet, a special yeast and the local spring waters of Shaoxing in northern China, where it is traditionally made. Used in myriad sauces and dressings, Shaoxing wine is available from the Asian section of supermarkets and at Asian grocery stores.

coconut

cream

The cream that rises to the top after the first pressing of coconut milk, coconut cream is higher both in energy and fat than regular coconut milk. It's a common ingredient in curries and Asian sweets. You can buy coconut cream in cans or cartons from most supermarkets.

desiccated

Desiccated coconut is coconut meat that has been shredded and dried to remove its moisture. It's unsweetened and very powdery. Great for baking as well as savoury Asian sauces and sambals.

flakes

Coconut flakes have a large shape and chewier texture than the desiccated variety, and are often used for decorating and in mueslis and baking. You can buy coconut flakes ready-toasted, with lovely golden edges, from supermarkets.

coconut milk

A milky, sweet liquid made by soaking grated fresh coconut flesh or desiccated coconut in warm water and squeezing it through muslin or cheesecloth. Coconut milk shouldn't be confused with coconut water, which is a clear liquid found inside young coconuts.

shredded

In slightly larger pieces than desiccated, shredded coconut is great for adding a bit more texture to slices and cakes, or for making condiments to serve with curries.

sugar

See *sugar (coconut)*, page 264.

yoghurt

Coconut yoghurt has become far more readily available in recent years, thanks to its dairy-free status. It's made from coconut milk and probiotic cultures. Find it in the chilled yoghurt section of most supermarkets and grocers.

coriander (cilantro)

This pungent green herb is common in Asian and Mexican cooking. The finely chopped roots are sometimes incorporated into curry pastes. The dried seeds can't be substituted for fresh coriander.

crème fraîche

A rich, tangy, fermented cream, traditionally from France, with a minimum fat content of 35 per cent. Available at grocers, delicatessens and most supermarkets.

dark chocolate

The dark chocolate called for in this book is 70% cocoa solids. Chocolate that has 70% cocoa solids is usually labelled as such, and has a more bitter, intense flavour and no powdery texture. It's sold in blocks and is ideal for use in baking. Find it in the baking aisle of supermarkets.

edamame

Find these tasty, tender soy beans ready-podded in the freezer section of major greengrocers, Asian grocers and some supermarkets.

They are a great addition to salads, stir-fries and pastas.

eggs

The standard egg size used in this book is 60g (2 oz). It's important to use the right sized eggs, for baking recipes especially, as it can affect the outcome. Room temperature eggs are best for baking.

fish sauce

This amber-coloured liquid drained from salted, fermented fish is used to add flavour to Thai, Vietnamese or Southeast Asian dishes, such as curries, noodles or salads, plus dressings and dipping sauces.

flaxseeds (linseeds)

These small brown seeds have a nutty flavour and are high in omega-3. They can be baked into bread, sprinkled in muesli and salads or used to make slices. Find them at supermarkets and health food stores

flour

brown rice flour

This gluten free flour is made from wholegrain brown rice and is used for thickening sauces, or in gluten free baking or pancake recipes. It has a mild nutty flavour. Find it at supermarkets or health food stores.

buckwheat

Despite its name, buckwheat flour isn't from a grain but is milled from the seed of a plant related to rhubarb and sorrel. Often used in pancakes and noodles for its rich, nutty flavour and wholesome benefits, it's also gluten free.

cornflour (cornstarch)

When made from ground corn or maize, cornflour is gluten free.

Recipes often require it to be blended with water or stock for use as a thickening agent. Not to be confused with cornflour in the United States, which is actually finely ground corn meal.

plain (all-purpose)
Ground from the endosperm of wheat, plain white flour contains no raising agent.

rice
Rice flour is a fine flour made from ground rice. Available in white and brown varieties, it's often used as a thickening agent in baking, in cookies and shortbreads, and to coat foods when cooking Asian dishes. It's gluten free and available in supermarkets and health food stores.

self-raising (self-rising)
Ground from the endosperm of wheat, self-raising flour contains raising agents including sodium carbonates and calcium phosphates.

spelt
Milled from the ancient cereal grain, spelt flour boasts more nutrients and is better tolerated by some than regular flour.

wholemeal (whole-wheat)
Ground from the whole grain of wheat and thus keeping more of its nutrients and fibre, this flour is available in plain (all-purpose) and self-raising (self-rising) varieties from most supermarkets and health food stores.

farro

Farro is an ancient variety of wheat that is sold dry and cooked in water. It has a firm, chewy texture and a light nutty flavour. Its flavour and firm texture make it a great addition to salads, risottos and soups. Farro can be found in supermarkets and health food stores. 1 cup cooked farro weighs 200g (7 oz). Directions for cooking farro are as follows.

1 cup (200g) farro
2½ cups (625ml) water
pinch of salt

Place the farro, salt and water in a medium saucepan over high heat. Bring to the boil, cover with a tight-fitting lid and reduce heat to medium-low. Cook for 15–20 minutes or until tender. Drain any remaining water. **MAKES 2½ CUPS (450G)**

freekeh

Freekeh is the immature or 'green' wheat grain that has been roasted. The recipes in this book call for whole-grain freekeh as opposed to cracked freekeh. The grains can be used in salads and tabouli or eat it as you would rice or pasta. Find it in supermarkets and health food stores. 1 cup cooked freekeh weighs 160g (5½ oz). Directions for cooking freekeh are as follows.

1 cup (220g) freekeh
3 cups (750ml) water

Place the freekeh and water in a medium saucepan over high heat. Bring to the boil, immediately cover with a tight-fitting lid and reduce the heat to low. Cook for 30–35 minutes or until tender. Drain any remaining water. **MAKES 3 CUPS (480G)**

furikake

This nutty, crunchy, flavourful Japanese seasoning is typically made from toasted sesame seeds, nori, salt and sugar. It is used widely in Japanese cuisine to season rice and noodles, but also adds great flavour and texture to pasta, proteins and stir-fries. Find it in the Asian section of the supermarket or in Asian supermarkets. If you can't find it, use shredded nori sheets and sesame seeds instead.

gai lan (chinese broccoli)

Also known as Chinese broccoli or Chinese kale, gai lan is a leafy vegetable with dark green leaves, tiny white or yellow flowers and stout stems. It can be steamed or blanched and served with oyster sauce as a simple side or added to soups, stir-fries and braises towards the end of the cooking time. Gai lan is sold in bunches at greengrocers and supermarkets.

gochujang

This is a spicy, savoury and slightly sweet red chilli paste originating in Korea, made from fermented rice, wheat and red chillies. Find it in the Asian section of the supermarket or in Asian supermarkets.

gow gee wrappers

Chinese in origin, these round, thin sheets of dough are available chilled or frozen. They can be steamed or fried. Fill them with meat and vegetables to make dumplings, or use as a crunchy base for nibbles.

green onions (scallions)

Both the white and green part of these long mild onions are used in salads, as a garnish and in Asian cooking. Sold in bunches, they give a fresh bite to dishes. Find them at the supermarket, Asian supermarkets or greengrocers.

hoisin sauce

This thick, sweet and salty sauce is used extensively in Chinese cuisine.

It is a dark soy-based sauce that can be used as a glaze, in sauces and as a dipping sauce. Find it in the Asian aisle in the supermarket.

horseradish

A pungent root vegetable that releases mustard oil when cut or grated, horseradish is available fresh from greengrocers. You can substitute it with pre-grated or creamed varieties sold in jars.

kaffir lime leaves

Also known as makrut lime, these fragrant leaves have a distinctive double-leaf structure. Commonly crushed or shredded and used as a garnish, the leaves are available fresh or dried, from most greengrocers and at Asian food stores. Fresh leaves are more flavourful and freeze well.

kecap manis

Also known as sweet soy sauce, kecap manis or ketjap manis is a type of soy sauce that originated in Indonesia. It is thicker and sweeter than soy sauce. Find it in the Asian food section of most supermarkets.

Lebanese cucumber

This sweet-flavoured, crisp-fleshed and smooth-skinned cucumber is featured throughout this book, and is used widely in salads. It is similar to the English cucumber, Persian cucumber and the American garden cucumber.

lemongrass

Lemongrass is a tall lemon-scented grass used in Asian cooking, mainly in Thai dishes. Peel away the outer leaves and chop the tender white root-end finely, or add in large pieces during cooking and remove before serving. If adding in larger pieces,

bruise them with the back of a kitchen knife. It is often used in curry pastes due to its fragrant, punchy flavour profile. Find it at supermarkets and greengrocers.

maple syrup

A sweetener made from the sap of the maple tree, be sure to use pure maple syrup. Imitation, or pancake syrup is made from corn syrup flavoured with maple and does not have the same intensity of flavour. The maple syrup referred to throughout this book is pure maple syrup, free from additives and preservatives.

mirin (Japanese rice wine)

Mirin is a pale yellow, sweet and tangy Japanese cooking wine made from glutinous rice and alcohol.

miso paste

Miso is a traditional Japanese ingredient produced by fermenting rice, barley or soy beans to a paste. It's used for sauces and spreads, pickling vegetables, and is often mixed with dashi stock to serve as miso soup. Sometimes labelled simply 'miso', white, yellow and red varieties are available, their flavour increasing in intensity with their colour. The recipes in this book call for white miso (shiro) for its delicate flavour and colour. Find miso paste in supermarkets and Asian grocers.

mizuna

Mizuna means 'water green' in Japanese. It is a mild flavoured Japanese mustard green that gives a slightly peppery kick to salads. Mizuna features dark green serrated leaves. It can be found at some greengrocers and farmer's markets. If you can't find it, regular mustard greens make a good substitute.

noodles

Most fresh noodles will keep in the fridge for up to a week. Keep a supply of dried noodles in the pantry for last-minute meals. Available from supermarkets and Asian food stores.

dried rice

Fine, dried (stick) noodles common in southeast Asian cooking. Depending on their thickness, rice noodles need only be boiled briefly, or soaked in hot water until soft.

rice vermicelli

Very thin dried rice noodles sometimes called rice sticks. They are usually used in soups such as laksa and in salads.

soba

Japanese noodles made from buckwheat and wheat flour, soba are greyish brown in colour and served in cold salads or in hot soups.

udon

This thick Japanese wheat noodle is commonly used in soups.

nori

Nori sheets are paper-thin layers of dried seaweed, commonly used for making sushi rolls. High in protein and minerals, nori can also be chopped or used as a garnish. Buy nori, ready-toasted if necessary, at most supermarkets and Asian grocers.

nutritional yeast

This is inactive yeast that is grown specifically to be used in food. It is a complete protein, so it's a great addition to a vegan diet. Nutritional yeast is called as such because it contains essential vitamins and minerals – it's high in B vitamins. It adds a savoury, umami flavour to dishes. Find it in the health food section of most supermarkets.

oil

extra virgin olive

Graded according to its flavour, aroma and acidity. Extra virgin is the highest-quality olive oil; it contains no more than 1% acid. Virgin is the next best; it contains 1.5% or less acid. Bottles labelled simply 'olive oil' contain a blend of refined and unrefined virgin olive oil. 'Light' olive oil is the least pure in quality and shouldn't be confused with light-flavoured extra virgin olive oil.

light-flavoured extra virgin olive

This is still the highest-quality olive oil and is made from a pure blend of the oil from milder-flavoured olives.

sesame

Pressed from sesame seeds, sesame oil is used in Asian cuisine more as a nutty, full-flavoured seasoning than a cooking medium.

vegetable

Oils sourced from plants or seeds, with very mild, unobtrusive flavours. Often called for in baking recipes or Asian dishes, for this reason. Look out for palm oil on the label of your oil.

panko

These breadcrumbs have a drier, flakier texture than regular breadcrumbs. Panko is widely used in Japanese cuisine and often produces a lighter, crunchier crumb on proteins and vegetables. Find it in the Asian section of supermarkets.

paprika, smoked

Unlike Hungarian paprika, the Spanish style, known as pimentón, is deep and smoky. It is made from smoked, ground pimento peppers and comes in varying intensities, from sweet and mild (dulce), bittersweet medium hot (agridulce) and hot (picante). The variety called for in this book is smoky-sweet.

pastry

Make your own or use one of the many store-bought varieties, including shortcrust and filo, which are sold frozen in blocks or ready-rolled into pastry sheets. Defrost in the fridge before use.

filo

This very thin, delicate pastry is known for crisping up well when baked in the oven. It is used widely in sweet and savoury dishes such as pies and baklava. In this book, we prefer using store-bought filo from the fridge section of the supermarket rather than frozen filo, as it's easier to work with. To keep filo from drying out, cover with a clean damp tea towel while it is out of the fridge.

puff and butter puff

This pastry is quite difficult to make, so many cooks opt to use store-bought puff pastry. It can be bought in blocks from patisseries, or sold in both block and sheet forms in supermarkets. Butter puff pastry is very light and flaky, perfect for savoury and sweet pies and tarts. Often labelled 'all butter puff', good-quality sheets are usually thicker. If you can only buy thin sheets, don't be afraid to stack 2 regular thawed sheets together.

pepitas (pumpkin seeds)

Pumpkin seeds are hulled to reveal these olive green kernels that, once dried, are nutty in flavour and easy to use in smoothies, baking and salads. Find them in supermarkets.

pickled ginger

Also known as gari, this Japanese condiment is made from young ginger that's been pickled in sugar and vinegar. It's commonly served with Japanese food as a palate cleanser, but is becoming popular as a tangy addition to sushi bowls and salads. Buy it in jars from Asian grocers and some supermarkets.

pomegranate molasses

A concentrated syrup made from pomegranate juice, with a sweet, tart flavour, pomegranate molasses is available from Middle Eastern grocery stores and specialty food shops. If you can't find it, try using caramelised balsamic vinegar.

porcini mushrooms

Available fresh in Europe and the UK and sold dried elsewhere, including Australia and the US. They have an almost meaty texture and earthy taste. Soak dried porcini mushrooms before using, and use the soaking liquid as a stock if desired. Frozen porcinis are becoming readily available. Like the dried variety, they're available from specialty food stores.

portobello mushroom

Portobello mushrooms are large, dark mushrooms with an open cap. They have a deep and 'meaty' mushroom flavour and are often used in burgers due to their size. Portobello mushrooms can also be baked, stuffed, fried or stir-fried. Find them at the green grocer.

quinoa

Packed with protein, this grain-like seed has a chewy texture, nutty flavour and is fluffy when cooked. Use it as you would couscous or rice. It freezes well, so any excess cooked quinoa can be frozen in individual portions. Red and black varieties, which require a slightly longer cooking time, are also available in most supermarkets. 1 cup cooked white quinoa weighs 160g (5½ oz). Directions for cooking quinoa are as follows.

1 cup (180g) white quinoa
1¼ cups (310ml) water
sea salt flakes

Place the quinoa, water and a pinch of salt in a medium saucepan over high heat. Bring to the boil, cover immediately with a tight-fitting lid and reduce the heat to low. Simmer for 12 minutes or until almost tender. Remove from the heat and allow to steam for 8 minutes or until tender. **MAKES 2¾ CUPS (440G)**

flakes
Quinoa flakes are simply quinoa seeds that have been steamrolled into flakes. Use them in muesli or baked goods, or as a healthier crumb coating for proteins. Find them in health food stores and the health food aisle of supermarkets.

rice
arborio
Rice with a short, plump-looking grain that cooks to a soft texture, while retaining a firm interior. It has surface starch that creates a creamy texture in risottos when cooked to al dente. It can also be used in rice pudding. Arborio is available at most supermarkets.

brown
Brown rice is different to white rice in that the bran and germ of the wholegrain are intact. This renders it nutritionally superior and gives it a nutty chewiness. It's available at

supermarkets. 1 cup cooked brown rice weighs 200g (7 oz). Directions for cooking brown rice are as follows.

1 cup (200g) brown rice
1½ cups (375ml) water
sea salt flakes

Place the rice, water and a pinch of salt in a medium saucepan over high heat. Bring to the boil, immediately cover with a tight-fitting lid and reduce the heat to low. Simmer for 25 minutes or until almost tender. Remove from the heat and allow to steam for 10 minutes or until tender. **MAKES 2 CUPS (400G)**

sage
This Mediterranean herb has a distinct, fragrant flavour and soft, oval-shaped grey-green leaves. It's used often in Italian cooking, crisped in a pan with butter or oil.

sesame seeds
These small seeds have a nutty flavour and can be used in savoury and sweet cooking. White sesame seeds are the most common variety, but black, or unhulled, seeds are popular for coatings in Asian cooking.

shiso leaves
Sometimes called perilla, this herb comes in both green and purple-leafed varieties. It has a slight peppery flavour and is often used to wrap ingredients. The micro variety makes a pretty garnish. Find it at some greengrocers and Asian markets.

silverbeet (swiss chard)
A vegetable with large, crinkly, glossy dark green leaves and prominent white, red or yellow stalks, silverbeet is rich in nutrients. It can be used in salads, soups, pies and steamed as a

side. Not to be confused with English spinach which has a smaller and more delicate leaf, silverbeet is best trimmed and washed before use.

sorrel leaves
This leafy green has a signature sour flavour. The red-veined leaves are a pretty and nutritious addition to salads. Find red-veined sorrel leaves at your local greengrocer.

sriracha hot chilli sauce
A hot sauce containing chilli, salt, sugar, vinegar and garlic, sriracha is both the brand name of a popular American blend as well as the generic name for the Southeast Asian sauce. Find it in supermarkets.

sugar
Extracted as crystals from the juice of the sugar cane plant, sugar is a sweetener, flavour enhancer and food preservative.

brown
In Australia, what is known as 'brown sugar' is referred to as 'light brown sugar' in other parts of the world. Light and dark brown sugars are made from refined sugar with natural molasses added. Light and dark types are interchangeable if either is unavailable. An important ingredient in cookies, puddings, dense cakes and brownies, you can find both varieties of brown sugar in supermarkets.

caster (superfine)
The superfine granule of caster sugar gives baked products a light texture and crumb, which is important for many cakes and delicate desserts. Caster sugar is essential for making meringue, as the fine crystals dissolve more easily in the whipped eggwhite.

coconut

With an earthy, butterscotch flavour, coconut sugar, or coconut palm sugar, comes from the flowers of the coconut palm. Coconut sugar gives a lovely depth of flavour. Find it in some supermarkets, specialty food shops, Asian grocers and health food stores.

demerara

Demerara is a coarse-grained golden cane sugar, with a mild molasses flavour. Like raw sugar, it's delicious stirred into coffee or sprinkled over baked treats for a sweet caramel crust.

icing (confectioner's)

Icing sugar is granulated sugar ground to a very fine powder. When mixed with liquid or into butter or cream cheese it creates a sweet glaze or icing, plus it can be sifted over cakes or desserts. Unless specified, use pure icing sugar, not icing sugar mixture, which contains cornflour (cornstarch) and needs more liquid.

raw (golden) caster

Light brown in colour and honey-like in flavour, raw sugar is slightly less refined than white sugar, with a larger granule. It lends a more pronounced flavour and colour to baked goods. You can use demerara sugar in its place.

sumac

These dried berries of a flowering plant are ground to produce an acidic, vibrant crimson powder that's popular in the Middle East. Sumac has a lemony flavour and is great sprinkled on salads, dips, yoghurt or chicken. Find it at greengrocers, specialty spice shops and some supermarkets.

sunflower seeds

These small grey kernels from the black and white seeds of sunflowers are mostly processed for their oil. The kernels are also found in snack mixes and muesli, and can be baked into breads and slices. Buy sunflower seeds in supermarkets.

tahini

A thick paste made from ground sesame seeds, tahini is widely used in Middle-Eastern cooking. It's available in jars and cans from supermarkets and health food stores, in both hulled and unhulled varieties. The recipes in this book call for hulled tahini, for its slightly smoother texture.

tofu

Not all tofu is created equal. The recipes in this book call for either firm or silken tofu, which can be found in the chilled section of the supermarket. Where possible, choose organic non-GMO tofu. All brands vary in texture and taste, so don't give up until you find one you love. It's a great source of protein and acts like a sponge for flavour.

vanilla

bean paste

This store-bought paste is a convenient way to replace whole vanilla beans and is great in desserts. One teaspoon of paste substitutes for one vanilla bean.

beans

These fragrant cured pods from the vanilla orchid are used whole, often split and the tiny seeds inside scraped into the mixture to infuse flavour into cream-based recipes.

extract

For a pure vanilla taste, use a good-quality vanilla extract, not an essence or imitation flavour. Vanilla extract features a rounded, rich vanilla flavour.

vinegar

apple cider

Made from apple must, apple cider vinegar has a golden amber colour and a sour appley flavour. Use it to make dressings, marinades and chutneys. The recipes in this book call for organic or unfiltered apple cider vinegar.

balsamic

Originally from Modena in Italy, there are many balsamics on the market ranging in quality and flavour. Aged varieties are preferable. A milder white version is also available, which is used where colour is important. Find it at supermarkets or specialty stores.

rice wine

Made from fermenting rice (or rice wine), rice wine vinegar is milder and sweeter than vinegars that are made by oxidising distilled wine or other alcohol made from grapes. Rice wine vinegar is available in white, black, brown and red varieties and can be found in supermarkets and Asian food stores.

wine

Both red and white wine can be distilled into vinegar. Use in dressings, glazes and preserved condiments such as pickles. Use it to make a classic French vinaigrette.

yoghurt, natural Greek-style

Recipes in this book call for natural, unsweetened full-fat Greek-style (thick) yoghurt. Buy it from the chilled aisle of the supermarket, checking the label for any unwanted sweeteners or artificial flavours.

thank you

Creating a cookbook is a huge undertaking. So much dedication, creativity and talent goes into bringing a book like *One Pan Perfect* to life, and I am in awe of the talent I've been lucky enough to surround myself with.

To the lovely Chris Court, your approach to capturing beautiful imagery has truly shone through in this book. While we didn't solve any global crisis issues, we did create something beautiful to warm the hearts and bellies of people all over the world, and that's pretty amazing. I'm sure I'll see you out on a mountain bike trail soon enough.

To my right-hand woman, Hannah Schubert, this book would not exist without your exceptional talent and unwavering dedication to the cause. Your ability to switch from senior designer to studio manager and everything in between is amazing. You are truly a star!

To my dearest Chi Lam, your attention to detail and ability to bring everything together into one cohesive masterpiece is truly remarkable. You are a dear friend and working with you again has been an absolute treat.

To my fabulous editor Mariam Digges, your beautiful words have perfectly captured what I envisaged for this book. Your insight and expertise has made it truly special and I am so grateful.

To my recipe testing dynamos, Jacinta Cannataci and Tina McLeish, what a team! Thank you for your incredible attention to detail while testing this book. Your dedication and love for food is inspiring. Keep doing what you do!

At HarperCollinsPublishers, many thanks to Catherine Milne, Jim Demetriou, Janelle Garside and Belinda Yuille for your trust and support in my vision for this book.

Thank you to my loyal brand partners: CSR, Glad to be Green®, Cobram Estate, Farmers Union, Miele and Estée Lauder.

My sincerest thanks to ceramicist Marjoke De Heer (@marjokedeheer), Angela Nicholson (@angela_nicholson_studio), Andrea Brugi (@artbrugi), The Drill Hall Emporium (@thedrillhallemporium) and Mud Australia (@mudaustralia). Your pieces have brought such beauty to this book.

A big thank you to Ross and Dan at Hale Imports for their generous supply of cast iron pans (@lodgecastiron_australia), and my beautiful knives (@shun.australia).

To the dh team, who keep the dream alive every day: Karen Hay, my numbers whiz and giver of sage advice. Morgan Mathers, sponsorship and collaborations manager and stellar recipe taste tester. And Lauren Gibb, my digital wunderkid – thank you for the support, positivity, expertise and laughs that always keep me feeling supported.

Last but not at all least, a huge thank you to my partner and two boys. Your support and love throughout the process means the world to me. To my family and my amazing friends – thank you, endlessly. None of this would be possible without you.

About
Donna

As Australia's *leading food editor* and BESTSELLING COOKBOOK AUTHOR, Donna Hay has made her way into the hearts (and *almost every home*) across the country.

An *international publishing phenomenon*, Donna's name is synonymous with accessible yet INSPIRATIONAL RECIPES and *stunning images*. Her acclaimed magazine notched up an INCREDIBLE 100 ISSUES and her best-selling cookbooks sold more than *seven million copies* worldwide.

The DONNA HAY BRAND goes beyond the printed page, featuring an *impressive digital presence*; a number of TELEVISION SERIES; branded merchandise; and a *baking mix range* in Australian supermarkets. Donna is the VERY PROUD MUM of two teenage boys, adores living near the ocean and *still loves cooking* every single day.

Connect with Donna anytime, anywhere...

www.donnahay.com

@donna.hay

pinterest.com/
donnahayhome

facebook.com/
donnahay